22.95

05—1049

W9-BBZ-459

ATTACK THE MESSENGER

ATTACK THE MESSENGER

HOW POLITICIANS TURN
YOU AGAINST THE MEDIA

CRAIG CRAWFORD

ROWMAN & LITTLEFIELD PUBLISHERS, INC.
Lanham • Boulder • New York • Toronto • Oxford

ROWMAN & LITTLEFIELD PUBLISHERS, INC.

Published in the United States of America
by Rowman & Littlefield Publishers, Inc.
A wholly owned subsidary of The Rowman & Littlefield Publishing Group, Inc.
4501 Forbes Boulevard, Suite 200, Lanham, Maryland 20706
www.rowmanlittlefield.com

P.O. Box 317, Oxford OX2 9RU, UK

British Library Cataloguing in Publication Information Available

Library of Congress Cataloging-in-Publication Data
Crawford, Craig, 1956–
  Attack the messenger : how politicians turn you against the media / Craig
Crawford.
    p. cm. -- (American political challenges)
  Includes bibliographical references and index.
  ISBN 0-7425-3816-8 (cloth : alk. paper)
1. Mass media--Political aspects--United States. I. Title. II. Series.
P95.82.U6C73 2005
302.23'0973--dc22
                                        2005001705

Printed in the United States of America

♾™ The paper used in this publication meets the minimum requirements of
American National Standard for Information Sciences—Permanence of Paper for
Printed Library Materials, ANSI/NISO Z39.48-1992.

Contents

Acknowledgments

I want to recognize and thank the critical assistance provided by David Blank, who edited copy and suggested improvements with extreme patience and attention to detail; Dawn Michelle Miller of the University of Virginia's Institute for Politics, whose timely and comprehensive research added meaningful context to several chapters; and Nicholas Thimmesch, who helped in developing the Media Resource Guide. Also, a special thanks to Diane Nine for putting this project together and guiding it to the finish line. Finally, thanks to my parents, Bill and Toby Crawford, for their unconditional support.

1

Turning the Tables

It is the day the politicians began to win the war against the media.

Vice President George H. W. Bush is in his Capitol Hill office. CBS News anchorman Dan Rather is in his New York City studio on 57th Street. It is January 25, 1988.

Both men are in familiar settings. Aides surround them. One of Rather's investigative producers has briefed him in the final moments before the anchorman conducts a live interview of Bush on the *CBS Evening News*.

CBS producers prepared for weeks to arm Rather with plenty of questions designed to grill Bush about his role in what had become another long-running Washington soap opera, the Iran-Contra scandal.

As vice president in Ronald Reagan's administration, Bush was a point man on foreign policy. His background as former chief of the Central Intelligence Agency and ambassador to China put him in the middle of the action.

But many questions remained unanswered about what Bush knew about the scheme to sell arms to Iran and use the money to help fund a war against communism in Nicaragua. Congress refused to clearly authorize the war, so the Reagan team tried many creative methods to pursue its aims in Central America.

By the time of the Bush–Rather interview, President Reagan had come clean. He acknowledged in a nationally televised address that his administration had done things he once claimed they had not done. But Bush's role was still a mystery. It remains so today.

Rather's team was determined to "put Bush through the wringer," as one producer put it. Some of the network's most talented producers and researchers devoted themselves to this one interview. Some at CBS worried that their colleagues were asking for trouble, that Rather would be seen as conducting a vendetta.

Bush knew he faced a crucial moment in his bid to win the presidency for himself, even though election day was over eight months away. For years now, the news media had dogged the Reagan White House with Iran-Contra revelations. A series of congressional investigations and an independent prosecutor's probe often led the evening news and the front pages of newspapers.

At moments, it even seemed that Reagan would face impeachment. It took his televised mea culpa to make that prospect go away.

So far, Bush had escaped harm. His campaign team decided that it was time to face an accuser and put the story behind him. Dan Rather's newscast was a fitting venue for this purpose.

Rather was regarded by conservatives as the poster child for liberal media bias. If Bush could survive this test, his advisers believed, he could put the Iran-Contra story away.

CBS producers who negotiated the ground rules of the interview in advance say they had made it clear that Bush's role in the Iran-Contra scandal would be fair game, even though Bush and his aides later would claim he was not told the subject would come up.[1]

The Bush team got its way on the ground rules. CBS wanted to tape the interview. But Bush's aides had no intention of allowing CBS to edit the interview. They wanted a live interview.

It turns out that the Bush camp had something more than avoiding network editors in mind.

This was not just about Bush establishing an early defense for any part he played in the scandal that nearly scuttled the presidency of his boss, Ronald Reagan. Bush's campaign team, led by legendary television producer Roger Ailes, already knew that most Americans cared little about the complex scheme to sell weapons to Iran and use the proceeds to pay for a war in Nicaragua that Congress would not fund.

For the Bush team, the coming interview with Rather was more about establishing what would become one of their main campaign themes: to run against the liberal media. And Dan Rather would be their foil, the most well-known emblem for a media establishment they would portray as out of sync with right-thinking Americans.

THE SETUP

Politicians in all systems of government have long yearned to muzzle the press. In dictatorships, they simply murder annoying reporters. In democracies, the silencing of critics must be a bit more on the symbolic side.

American politicians have fought the press since the nation began. Thomas Jefferson, whose personal life provided plenty of fodder for malicious media gossip, once said, "The man who reads nothing at all is better educated than the man who reads nothing but newspapers."[2]

George Bush won the presidency in 1988 partly by targeting the news media. He and his aides in the Republican camp correctly believed that the media establishment, based in New York City and Washington, D.C., was comprised mostly of Democrats. The Bush camp believed the news media was out to get him after eight years of trying to bring down the Reagan administration on many fronts, including the controversial Iran-Contra scandal.

The 1988 Bush campaign skillfully deployed a number of techniques to subdue the news media. They turned the tables, making news media personalities and their bias the issue instead of the other way around. In the decades since, politicians in both parties learned to turn the tables on reporters, casting doubt on their motives and credibility.

In many ways, we had it coming. Biased or superficial reporting happens, endangering public trust.

But the political war on the media is about more than rooting out bad journalism. It is about politicians hoping to control information. They start by controlling—or at least subduing—the news media.

Since the 1988 presidential campaign, Democrats and Republicans learned to perfect the techniques of media manipulation. Bill Clinton survived a personal scandal by vilifying the messenger—the reporters who uncovered his sexual affair while in office. Bush's son, George W. Bush, took the nation to war in Iraq with little public debate, thanks in part to a muzzled press.

THE STING

On that January night in 1988, when the elder Bush and anchorman Dan Rather tangled, the public's perception of the media began a decades-long transformation. Bush wielded the most basic weapon in targeting the media—make the reporter the issue.

Bush took the offensive at the very start of the interview, which included a CBS News report about questions surrounding Bush's role in the Iran-Contra scandal.

"You've impugned my integrity by suggesting, with one of your little boards here, that I didn't tell the truth," Bush said before Rather could complete his first question.[3]

And before Rather could get his next line of questions out, Bush fired back by reminding Rather of a time when the anchorman walked off his own set out of anger at the preemption of his show for a sporting event.

"I want to talk about why I want to be president," Bush said. "It's not fair to judge my whole career by a rehash on Iran. How would you like it if I judged your career by those seven minutes when you walked off the set in New York?"[4]

It was not an offhand remark. It was on a cue card.

Bush's campaign manager, Roger Ailes—a burly force of nature who would go on to revolutionize television news at the helm of the Fox News Channel—was holding the cue card. And he had to write the card in fist-size letters.

Longtime CBS camera operator George Christian, who ran the camera on Bush that day, was surprised to see an aide prompting answers with a cue card during a live news interview. "I had never seen that before," Christian said.[5]

Christian said that CBS producers instructed him to place his camera unusually far away from Bush for the interview. Producers expected that the vice president might walk out. They wanted their camera operator to be able to air any walkout live on the broadcast.

Ailes stood next to the camera operator, some thirty feet away from Bush. At the moment he wanted Bush to go on the attack, he held up a poster with a handwritten message. "NOW ASK," the homemade cue card began. It went on to prompt Bush to refer to an incident when Rather walked off his own set.

The year before, Rather had walked off the anchor desk before a live broadcast, angry about a network decision to continue carrying a tennis match that ran past the time when he was scheduled to be on the air. When the match ended and Rather was supposed to come on the air, CBS local stations were on their own for seven minutes.

Many television news executives considered Rather's behavior unprofessional. It was another in a long series of incidents that exposed his emotional side.

Rather's tendency to interject his feelings into his work made him a perfect target for the Bush team. Not only could they divert attention from the story Rather was pursuing, but they could rally conservative voters to Bush's side. Many conservatives were unsure that Bush was hard-line enough for them. The word "wimp" was often used in referring to Bush, a mild-mannered gentleman who often gave the impression of someone more comfortable on a country club tennis court than in the bare-knuckled fray of political warfare.

In short, Bush needed to prove his manhood. He needed to pick a fight.

Rather first made himself a conservative target during Richard Nixon's presidency.

As CBS's White House correspondent during the Nixon years, Rather was a bulldog on the Watergate story that ended in the first-ever presidential resignation.

Many Republicans thought Rather crossed the line with a provocative question that led to a famous exchange with Nixon during a presidential press conference in March 1974.

Rather: "Mr. President, I wonder if you could share with us your thoughts, tell us what goes through your mind when you hear people, people who love this country and people who believe in you, say reluctantly that perhaps you should resign or be impeached?"

Nixon: "Well, I am glad we don't take the vote of this room, let me say."

The two often sparred. After one testy exchange with his nemesis, Nixon really got personal.

"Are you running for something?" Nixon asked.

Rather's response earned him a permanent spot in the archives of television news:

"Mr. President, are you?"

Although delivered in a respectful tone, Rather's point was clear. Nixon was losing his presidency despite his recent reelection. The president was so unpopular that he was running for office all over again, Rather implied.

From that moment on, Rather was on the Republican hit list.

Although he had moved on to the *CBS Evening News* anchor desk by the time Republicans regained control of the White House with Ronald Reagan, he was Enemy No. 1. Leslie Stahl, the CBS White House correspondent in those years, said Rather was "a man many in the White House saw as the devil himself."

This is where things stood between Rather and the Republicans when Bush stepped into his vice presidential office in 1988. He was there to slay the dragon.

Bush came to the interview in need of a macho moment. After eight years as Reagan's understudy, some in his own party feared he did not have the right stuff. He was still smarting from a *Newsweek* magazine cover that questioned his manhood with a picture of him under some fighting words: "Fighting the Wimp Factor."

That *Newsweek* headline was mischievously timed to hit the stands on the day that Bush announced his bid for the presidency. It infuriated his family and staff, forever hardening their relations with the news media. Bush had allowed the magazine's reporter, Margaret Warner, to travel with him behind the scenes as she worked on the upcoming article, granting closer access than anyone in the news media had gotten during his years in the Reagan White House.

Warner's *Newsweek* profile was mostly sympathetic. If not for the cover headline, it would have been an overall plus for the Bush campaign. But she did address the widely held view that he was too timid for the presidency, labeling it a "potentially crippling handicap."[6]

Years later, Warner blamed her editors for jazzing up the story and cover headline with the word "wimp." Now a PBS anchor, she told Ken Auletta of the *New Yorker* magazine in 2004 that the "Wimp Factor" headline was a "cruel, gratuitous thing" for editors to do. She said the Bush family let her know they were "hurt and irate."[7]

Fallout from the *Newsweek* cover story continued for weeks. The magazine surfaced an angle that many in Washington had privately discussed since it became clear that Bush would seek the White House on his own. Many Republicans, and more than a few in the Reagan administration, confirmed the *Newsweek* take on Bush's supposed testosterone deficiency. Now it was fair game for news commentators and others to openly call Bush a wimp who could not win the presidency. It had become the "crippling handicap" that *Newsweek* prophesied.

Bush's fateful interview with Dan Rather came just three months after the *Newsweek* slam on his manliness. Getting tough with Rather on the air would go a long way toward proving that the vice president was tough enough for a promotion.

Moments before Rather began asking questions, it was clear that Bush was in a feisty mood. As the network went to commercial just before the interview was to begin, CBS ran a "tease" of the coming interview. It promised a hard look at Bush's role in the Iran-Contra scandal.

"That's not what I'm here for," Bush said during the break, after hearing the promo. "If it's all on that, they're going to find a seven-minute walk-out here."[8]

Although Bush and his team claimed they didn't expect the Iran-Contra focus, CBS producers who negotiated the interview say they made it clear that the topic would come up. And the network had promoted the interview on earlier broadcasts, clearly stating that Bush's record on Iran-Contra would be examined.[9]

Still, the network had not made its focus clear in a letter to the Bush campaign requesting the interview. Instead, the written request established the interview as one of a "series of candidate profiles" to be included in "our early coverage of the 1988 presidential election."

The letter, from CBS producer Richard M. Cohen, noted that "Dan Rather is very interested in your profile and has decided to do it himself." "Mr. Rather," the letter said, "feels that because you are the incumbent Vice President and a front-runner that your candidacy deserves special attention."

Despite the vagueness of the written interview request, the Bush campaign could not reasonably think that such an interview would skip over the Iran-Contra scandal. But CBS did not make it clear that the topic would dominate the interview and the taped report leading into it.

Bush was obviously prepped to react strongly. He had already threatened to walk out in his off-air comments. The fireworks began just seconds into the live interview.

Right on cue, Bush delivered the lines that his manager, Roger Ailes, prompted with his handwritten poster.

Bush: "How would you like it if I judged your career by those seven minutes when you walked off the set in New York?"

From that point, the interview disassembled into a verbal shoving match between the two. At several points they talked over each other, including this exchange:

> Bush: I've answered every question put before me. Now if you have
> a question, please.
> Rather: I do have one.
> Bush: Please.
> Rather: I have one.
> Bush: Please fire away.
> Rather: You have said that if you had known this was an arms-for-
> hostages swap that you would have opposed it. You also said that . . .
> Bush: Exactly.
> Rather: . . . that you did not know.
> Bush: May I answer that.
> Rather: That wasn't the question, it was a statement . . .
> Bush: It was a statement . . .
> Rather: Let me ask the question, if I may, first.[10]

Bush was pleased with himself after the interview. "Well, I had my say," he blurted, pulling the earpiece and microphone off. Bush walked over to greet supporters who had been in the room saying, "He didn't lay a glove on me." CBS employees overheard him demean Rather with an off-color slang term for the female anatomy.[11]

Over his shoulder, the vice president shouted an ominous threat to CBS workers in the room. "Tell your goddamned network that if they want to talk to me to raise their hands at a press conference. No more Mr. Inside stuff after that."

Despite the show of anger, Bush saw the encounter's positive effect.

"It's going to help me," Bush told his well-wishers.

He was correct.

THE FALLOUT

The upshot of this interview is how the personal clash between Bush and Rather became the whole story in the days that followed. Bush completely succeeded in derailing CBS plans to embarrass him with searing questions about Iran-Contra.

The topic of Iran-Contra was lost in the news coverage of the interview, which suited the Bush campaign's purposes.

"Rather's Questioning of Bush Sets Off Shouting on Live Broadcast," *The New York Times* headline read the next day over a story that included very little on the intended substance of the interview.[12]

The phone lines at CBS's Washington Bureau lit up like nothing anyone had ever seen. Most callers expressed outrage at Rather's treatment of Bush. The callers seemed to be well orchestrated. Some at CBS News believe the Bush campaign prompted supporters to besiege the network's phone lines.[13]

Local CBS stations around the country reported an unprecedented wave of calls, mostly from angry viewers who said Rather was disrespectful to the vice president.

A news director for a South Carolina CBS affiliate told reporters there "wasn't one positive call" supporting Rather. "I've been in the business for twenty years and I don't remember any reaction as strong as this one," he said.[14]

Rather took a severe beating for his role in the meltdown of a network interview. Many at CBS News wanted the network to defend itself. Some thought it would be wise to put the word out that Bush's campaign manager was standing there with a cue card prompting the vice president to launch a personal attack on Rather.

Rather was getting blamed for starting the fight, even though CBS staffers with the vice president insisted to their bosses that Bush was responsible. Network chiefs decided to limit their response to a written statement asserting that its producers had told Bush aides that the interview would be "issue-oriented and tough."

While CBS remained silent on what its employees had witnessed off the air, the Bush campaign successfully put their stamp on the episode. To their side, it was another case of the liberal news media unfairly attacking Republicans.

Consequently, there were few hints in the news coverage that it was a setup, that Bush attacked Rather to divert attention from an important story and make himself a hero to conservatives.

The fallout of this interview goes beyond the personal. It symbolized the start of a turning of the tables. Never before had anyone, especially a politician of Bush's stature, gone ballistic on a network anchor. Bush pulled the pedestal away that night.

The news media had become too arrogant. The godlike worship of network anchors was silly, and Rather was a perfect foil. But the consequences of what Bush began that night go beyond taking the elite media down a notch or two.

MEDIA ON THE RUN

In the years since the Bush–Rather meltdown, the vilification of the news media by politicians has diminished the power of an independent press.

Bush challenged Rather in a way that undermined the role of a journalist to stand in the shoes of average citizens who cannot get personal interviews with political leaders and ask the questions those leaders prefer not to answer.

And once the dust settled on this incident, the American people still had no meaningful answers from a politician who did have some explaining to do. To this day, the extent of Bush's participation in a rogue foreign policy is still not established.

Until the Bush–Rather interview, the standard technique for not answering an unwelcome question in such a high-profile setting would be to change the subject and talk about something else. But politicians know that the public has grown more savvy about seeing through that ruse.

Buoyed by their success against Rather, the Bush 1988 campaign went on to demonize the media in other ways.

When questions were raised about the slim qualifications of Bush's running mate choice, Dan Quayle, the Bush team set up the entire campaign press corps.

In the days after the Republican nominating convention, the Bush campaign took Quayle to his hometown in Huntington, Indiana, for a rally and for the new running mate's first exposure to a media grilling.

Questions about Quayle's military record were especially hot on this day. Charges were flying that Quayle used his wealthy family's influence to avoid service in Vietnam by joining the National Guard.

Residents of Quayle's hometown, a farming community of about 16,000 people eighty miles northeast of Indianapolis, seemed the perfect backdrop for a press conference, in the view of his campaign handlers.

After first saying there would be no Quayle press conference anytime soon, the Bush team suddenly announced one to the traveling press. They would get the press conference they had been clamoring for, and not only that, they would get it in a matter of minutes.

Quayle was quickly hooked up to a public address system near his hometown crowd. His aides made sure the crowd could hear it all.

Predictably, the first question from the media was about whether he had used influence to get into the National Guard. The question wasn't fully asked before the crowd started booing.

The crowd got so loud and feisty that many reporters could not hear the questions or the answers. Angry about the chaotic circumstances of this first opportunity to ask Quayle about this story, some of the reporters got nasty.

Ellen Hume of the *Wall Street Journal* asked Quayle how he felt when "people were dying in Vietnam while you were writing press releases." That question provoked some in the crowd to start hurling personal insults at Hume.[15]

It was another legendary moment for the campaign that began to turn the tables on the news media. In this episode, the Bush campaign had actually found a way to unleash an angry mob against reporters. And that was the image that flashed across the screens of television news coverage.[16]

As always happens when the news media is attacked, it was the news media itself that relayed the images and words of its own demise. While there were furious conversations between the traveling press and Bush aides over the decision to put the Quayle press conference on a public address system, the rest of the nation was left with the sight and sound of average Americans yelling at the media.

In the years since, the yelling just got louder. The Bush 1988 presidential campaign was the turning point.

Politicians in both political parties learned from the Bush 1988 team how to run against the press. For now, the politicians have the upper hand.

It has been a long slide downhill since the zenith of press power, when the Watergate scandal ousted Nixon.

Nearly fifteen years later, Bush's televised meltdown with Rather and the public spectacle of Quayle's first national press conference served as the opening shots in a war between politicians and the media.

The politicians won.

2

Blame the Messenger

Politicians won the war against the media with a simple rule: first, attack the messenger.

The modern era of American politicians subduing the media began in 1988 with the election of the first President Bush. He ran against the liberal-leaning base of the national media establishment and won.

Liberals also attack the media. Former Vermont Governor Howard Dean, a liberal Democrat, had this to say after losing his 2004 bid for the presidency: "The media is a failing institution in this country. They are not maintaining their responsibility to maintain democracy."[1]

Dean's criticism is ironic. It was the media that made him famous. He rose to the top of the heap in the year before the 2004 Democratic primaries, thanks largely to the campaign press corp's fascination with his dark horse, Internet-based candidacy. He was even dubbed the front-runner before a single vote was cast.

But it was also the media that knocked him down after his loss in the first voting contest, the Iowa caucuses in January 2004. The news media obsessed on the intensity of Dean's feisty concession speech on caucus night, intended to rally hundreds of disappointed but still enthusiastic supporters. The "Dean scream," as it was labeled, was roundly criticized as a sign that the energetic politician might be a bit loopy.

Dean never recovered from the moment. His trajectory is a cautionary tale for politicians who rely too much on so-called media momentum in campaigns. As the saying goes, "If you live by the tube, you die by the tube."

It is, therefore, not unusual that Dean ended up so bitter about the media's role. Politicians almost instinctively blame the media when things go wrong.

Attacking the messenger always finds a receptive audience.

It's human nature. When you don't want to believe something, what do you do? First, you blame the messenger.

If the doctor has bad news, get a second opinion. If your bank statement doesn't balance, maybe it's the bank's fault. If you get a bad grade in school, the teacher is out to get you.

Got a bad review at work? The boss just doesn't understand you.

Sometimes the messenger is wrong. But many times you eventually have no choice but to accept what you do not want to hear.

So it is with the news. If you don't like what you read on the front page of your newspaper, maybe the reporter is biased or just plain stupid. If the evening news on television doesn't please you, blame the messenger.

Consuming news with skepticism is a good thing. Plenty of reporting is biased, misinformed, and, yes, just plain stupid.

But these days, public distrust of the news media is at a dangerously high point. Our instincts to blame the messenger are confirmed again and again.

A *New York Times* reporter is fired for making up stories.

A *USA Today* reporter and several editors are fired for a series of plagiarism incidents over a number of years.

CBS News executives are forced to admit that *60 Minutes* producers relied on a forged document to question a president's military service record.

Online news is no exception. Often, you can bet that if a story is only online, it's probably wrong.

We're still waiting for the pictures of George Bush dancing naked on a bar table. Years ago, Web newsies breathlessly reported we'd soon see them.

Sometimes, however, it is a story so hot or troubling that the mainstream media does not want to touch it.

Word of Bill Clinton's sexual affair in the White House first circulated on the Internet. Even when a major newsmagazine finally decided to run the story, it leaked onto the Web before it was published.

Thanks to the Internet and its Net-citizen journalists known as bloggers, anyone with a modem can spread lies or truth. It is often difficult to know the difference.

The old ways of journalism are long gone—and for good. There was a time when a handful of elites in New York City and Washington, D.C., set the news agenda.

A network news chief riding to work in his limousine would read the *New York Times* and take his cues for what would lead the evening news. A president or his top aides could call an influential reporter for a major newspaper and feed him a story that would drive the next day's news cycle.

As radio personality Don Imus once said of top news chiefs, "They write the news for their friends."[2]

THE DOWNSIDE OF THE MEDIA'S FALL

But all is not good in the demise of professionals in the news business. That same reporter who got the president's scoop one day could just as easily turn around and raise important questions about a political leader's decisions that fostered positive change.

Despite their faults, those who once set the national news agenda were committed to telling the truth. Maybe it was the truth as they saw it, and sometimes they delivered it with a left-leaning bias. But they did not deliberately spread lies.

Whatever their faults, the old gatekeepers of real news are gone. They needed a head knocking, and they got it. But what's replaced them presents a challenge, if not a threat, to democracy.

While there is more news to consume, there is no longer a consensus for truth in the news media. The major news organizations are under siege. They've been replaced by an agenda-driven rabble of pseudo-journalists on the Web and on cable news networks. There are few outlets anyone can trust to give unbiased information.

The role of the news media as an honest broker is shattered. The American people do not trust mainstream news sources anymore. Instead, they are drawn to sources that tell them what they want to hear.

In the 2004 presidential campaign, Internet bloggers on each side spread ridiculous lies about the opposing side's candidate. Hateful words and made-up stories filled the partisan websites. Rabid Democrats insisted that Bush and Cheney sent young Americans to their death in Iraq just to make money for Halliburton, the military services company that Cheney once ran. Equally rabid Republicans insisted that Kerry deliberately shot himself in Vietnam to win a war medal.

The ideological zealots who spread such claims blamed media bias for any attempts by legitimate news outlets to debunk unfounded charges against either candidate. Supporters who believed the claims were primed to ignore mainstream reporting, instead putting their faith in baseless rumors spread on the Internet.

I know. I get their e-mail. Writing a campaign column during the 2004 campaign for *Congressional Quarterly*, I got plenty of hate mail from both sides any time I struggled to play referee in the war of words and gossip between Internet bloggers for President George Bush and Democratic nominee John Kerry.

After my column on Kerry's war record, a man in Florida wrote, "Go back to your liberal hole." A Kerry supporter didn't like my comments on television about Bush's skillful handling of relief to Florida hurricane victims. "How dare you get on national television and talk out your ass," she wrote.

I would not pretend that my own e-mail is all that telling, but over the years I have noticed a remarkable increase in the hateful tone of reader responses. As a reporter and columnist since 1985, I have always given readers a way to contact me, and I usually write back. The advent of e-mail made this much easier.

Even if the message to me is full of venomous insults, I try to write a courteous response. Generally, I find that when I respond to a hateful message, an amazing thing happens. The writer backs down. It is almost as if they suddenly realize that they are not corresponding with the headless beast they imagined when originally writing. They discover that a real person with feelings is on the other end.

"Thank you for your polite and kind response," a Kerry supporter in Massachusetts wrote after originally accusing me of being "stupid," "silly," and "drunk" in a column criticizing the Democrat's performance at his national convention. "I still disagree, but I apologize for the shrillness before."

Still, this woman's original attitude represents the way in which a growing number of Americans see the news media—as stupid, silly, or just plain drunk. Maybe we deserve such harsh language, but the coarsening of attitudes toward the news media has broken what should be a natural bond between journalists and citizens.

BRING BACK BELIEVABLE REPORTING

Public distrust of the news media is one of the most hazardous political challenges now facing Americans. The need for believable reporting is even more critical in a time of war. A fearful public is more willing to give politicians a free hand to keep secrets, restrict liberties, and send our soldiers to their deaths—all in the name of national security.

The dethronement of news elites divided and conquered a once-powerful force in American life. At the peak of their power in the 1960s, they made a nation in denial see the tragic path our political leaders had led us into during the Vietnam War. A few years later, they toppled a president with the Watergate scandal.

Richard Nixon tried to run against the press. He routinely blamed the media for his problems.

After losing two elections in a row—the 1960 presidential race and his 1962 bid for governor of California—Nixon attacked the media during a stormy news conference.

On November 6, 1962, Nixon suffered a humiliating loss for the California governorship to Democrat Edmund "Pat" Brown. The next morning, he conceded defeat in one of the most bitter speeches of his political career. Blaming a biased press, Nixon announced that he was leaving politics.

Nixon started this press conference proclaiming that he had "no complaints about the press coverage" of the race he had just lost. "I will never complain about it," Nixon said. "I think that each of you were . . . was . . . writing it as you believed it, and I want that always to be the case in America."[3]

But he could not help himself. Nixon clearly believed the press coverage had been biased in favor of his Democratic opponent. He ended the press conference with a rambling diatribe against the media and a kicker line often replayed through the years.

"You don't have Nixon to kick around anymore," he told the reporters, "because gentlemen, this is my last press conference."[4]

Nixon's comments leading up to that closing line also should be remembered. He bared his true feelings about the media in a way that most politicians—Democrats or Republicans—would do if they let themselves:

> My philosophy with regard to the press has never really gotten
> through. And I want to get it through. This cannot be said for any
> other American figure today, I guess. Never in my sixteen years of
> campaigning have I complained to a publisher, to an editor, about

the coverage of a reporter. I believe a reporter has got a right to write it as he feels it. I believe that if a reporter believes that one man ought to win rather than the other, whether it's a television or radio or the like, he ought to say so. I will say to the reporter sometimes that I think, well look, well, look, I wish you'd give my opponent the same going-over that you give me. And as I leave the press, all that I can say is this: For sixteen years, ever since the Hiss case, you've had a lot of fun. A lot of fun. You've had an opportunity to attack me, and I think I've given as good as I've taken.[5]

One line in Nixon's speech especially stands out for me: "I believe that if a reporter believes that one man ought to win rather than the other, whether it's a television or radio or the like, he ought to say so," Nixon said.

I agree.

It is time for the news media to rethink what objectivity means. Concealing bias has left the media open to attack. The public, egged on by politicians, does not believe that reporters have no opinions.

Not revealing those opinions provokes politicians and critics to look for clues. Their imaginations run wild.

Would then–Vice President Bush have been able to put Rather on the defensive in their 1988 confrontation if Rather had made it clear he was opposed to Bush's election that year? Perhaps by clearing the decks on that score, Rather could have kept the interview focused on Bush's record. The public would have been better served. Instead, they got a juvenile shouting match that illuminated nothing.

Nixon's frustration was much like Bush's on the night of his Rather interview. When reporters with a bias appear to be pushing a political agenda in the guise of objective reporting, the politician under attack feels licensed to return fire.

In Nixon's case, his tortured feelings about the media ultimately brought him down. In 1962, when he said the media "won't have Nixon to kick around anymore," he was wrong on both counts.

Around six years later, he was running for president, and the media kicked him mercilessly. He resigned the presidency in August 1974.

ARROGANCE IS A BLINDING WEAKNESS

The moment Nixon resigned was the peak of press power. While many reveled in the moment as an example of the constitutionally protected media doing its job, Nixon's demise sowed the seeds of the media's demise.

By the time George H. W. Bush and his brilliant media handlers came along in 1988, the media had become arrogant to a fault.

Many in the top ranks of media organizations were beat reporters during Watergate. Many, like Rather, had played key roles in Nixon's undoing.

And many of them had just spent several years trying to take down Ronald Reagan over the Iran-Contra episode. They were determined to finish the job by preventing Bush's rise to the presidency.

What happened to the media in the years since highlights what the great American historian Charles A. Beard once said, "Whom the gods would destroy, they first make mad with power."[6]

Arrogance is a blinding weakness.

For more than a decade after the 1988 campaign, politicians and their friends conducted a full assault on "liberal media." The Bush family made it a personal crusade. Clinton perfected some of their techniques when faced with coverage of his personal life. A new cable outlet, the Fox News Channel, pursued and found a winning audience of those who believed the media was biased against conservatives.

Bush's 1988 campaign manager, Roger Ailes, took his expertise from that campaign right into the belly of the beast. He launched the Fox News Channel under the rousing banner, "We Report, You Decide." Fox soon dominated cable news, dethroning CNN. Once again, Ailes had the "liberal media" on the run.

All the while, those in charge of major news organizations looked on these developments with unconcerned amusement. Even today, many are still dismissive. But most know they've been had.

ABC News President David Westin spoke for his peers in observing that network news operations lost their way with viewers.

"The audience wants us to come to them, instead of making them come to us, which is traditionally what network news has done," Westin said at a Stanford University panel of network news chiefs after the 2004 presidential election.[7]

CBS News President Andrew Heyward agreed and tried to make the best of it.

"It's very different from the comfortable oligopoly that prevailed at the beginning of broadcast news, where you had networks with enormous market share," Heyward said. "I think that's to the public benefit. It puts more pressure on us to be excellent."[8]

The numbers tell the story.

The Gallup polling organization routinely monitors public faith in media as an institution. Not surprisingly, public support peaked during Watergate. In those days, more than 70 percent of the public trusted the media. Today, that number hovers around 50 percent.[9]

MEDIA WIMPS

The wimp factor is the most disturbing consequence of this trend. Today, reporters are less eager to stand up to power.

When real questions emerged about balloting problems in the 2004 presidential election, the mainstream news media took a pass. Few wanted to appear to be questioning the legitimacy of George W. Bush's reelection, especially after the debacle of the 2000 recount in Florida.

But the story was worth pursuing. Not because the election was stolen. It wasn't. The story was worth reporting because it showed how elections could be stolen.

In Ohio, for example, one county barred the press from the room where votes were counted. Electronic balloting machines around the country malfunctioned in mysterious ways. Internet bloggers had the story largely to themselves, which only muddied the waters. There was little reliably accurate reporting on it in the days right after the election.

Television host Keith Olbermann almost stood alone for weeks in his dogged reporting of the Ohio voting debate. Night after night on his MSNBC show, the broadcaster kept a tight focus on the story. Conservative pundits like Ann Coulter blasted him for it. He was accused of trying to overturn the election.

But the Ohio story was worth pursuing. There were lawsuits, voting recounts, congressional hearings, the works. Yet most of the news media barely touched it.

Olbermann wrote a daily online blog of his own chronicling his work on the story. He neatly explained his point in following the saga.

"Logic must suggest to the more sober of the Republicans that this needs to be addressed now," Olbermann wrote. He warned of the "potential for long-term damage that continuing a stonewall can wreak."[10]

Still, Olbermann's efforts to examine an important story put him at the top of the hate list in Republican and conservative circles.

Coulter devoted a column on her website to trashing what she called "Olbermann's idiotic conspiracy theory."

The Ohio voting problems turned out to be far more than conspiracy theories. Yet most of the mainstream media wimped out on this story largely because the Democrats did not immediately challenge the election. The coverage only stepped up once the Green Party and Libertarian Party exercised their rights under state law to request a recount of Ohio ballots.

This is a trend. Too often the media waits for the partisans in a dispute to carry a story forward. The news media seldom takes the lead or sticks with it when powerful politicians might be offended. They prefer to hide behind the charges of political opponents.

STANDING UP TO POWER

Today's media is as bullied as ever. Politicians don't have to dodge the tough questions anymore. They seldom even get them. Right or wrong, it is important and healthy for our politicians to be tested.

Before the Iraq War in 2003, most reporters in the White House press corps seldom challenged the president. A standout exception is longtime reporter Helen Thomas, who embodied the purpose—and the peril—of a free press in testy exchanges with President Bush and his advisers during televised press conferences. At the time, *Vanity Fair* magazine dubbed Thomas the "outlaw granny" of the press corps.[11] Even war supporters should have wanted answers to the questions she asked.

Only the free press can make politicians accountable. The founders of our nation understood this. They lived under an oppressive regime that jailed those who printed what it didn't want people to know. That is why they wrote a constitution that ranks freedom of the press in the top tier of rights for our democracy.

"Congress shall make no law respecting an establishment of religion, or prohibiting the free exercise thereof; or abridging the freedom of speech, or of the press; or the right of the people peaceably to assemble, and to petition the government for a redress of grievances."— First Amendment, Bill of Rights, U.S. Constitution.

Those who helped write the First Amendment deeply believed that freedom of the press was nonnegotiable.

"The liberty of the press is indeed a blessing, which ought not to be surrendered but with blood," wrote Edmund Randolph in a letter to James Madison in 1789.[12]

Without a free press, there is no freedom. Politicians everywhere—and throughout history—want to control the press and thereby control what the public knows about their deeds.

Thanks to the world's most protective constitution, the press in America is technically as free as it gets.

But politicians have found a way to limit the public benefits of our free press. They turned Americans against the news media, aided and abetted by the arrogance of elites in the news business who didn't know what hit them.

While network bosses and editors at major newspapers looked the other way, thinking their power was untouchable, politicians joined forces with talk radio giants like Rush Limbaugh. Together, they provoked millions of Americans to see the mainstream media as an enemy of their culture and values.

News chiefs made it easy for the politicians to bring them down. Many harbor an elitist view of Main Street America. Bad behavior and bias exist. But rooting out pervasive elitism and lousy journalism is not the only motivation for many of the politicians who target the press.

The truth threatens many politicians. They try to control what we think is true. They define truth on their own terms, which often is not the truth at all. As President Bill Clinton once famously said, "It depends on what the meaning of *is* is."

By undermining the credibility of the news media, politicians get the upper hand in defining what "is." Far from targeting only bad actors, these politicians seek to undermine our best journalists in hopes of muzzling the truth.

It is time for more Americans to appreciate a truly free and genuinely fair media and to demand more of it. Most reporters are trying to realize the promise of a free press: to bring you more truth than the politicians do.

Beware politicians and their friends who tell you to ignore the media. They might be hoping to make you believe their own lies.

Journalists are easy political targets because we seldom defend ourselves. We are trained to avoid making ourselves the story. We are supposed to cover the news makers and keep our own personalities and opinions out of the story. When politicians make us the story, we aren't sure how to handle it.

That is why CBS News executives mostly kept silent in 1988 after then–Vice President Bush attacked their anchor on the air. Network employees who had been with Bush in his office during the explosive interview implored their bosses to respond more forcefully.

Some at CBS felt it was worth noting in public that Bush launched his attack on Dan Rather from a cue card held up by his campaign manager. Veteran news personnel in the room had never seen such a thing. It made Bush's outburst seem orchestrated. Had that been publicized, Rather might not have been so widely criticized as the villain in this episode.

But CBS chose to issue a single written statement asserting that the Bush campaign had plenty of notice that Iran-Contra would be a topic in the interview. As a result, Bush and his supporters enjoyed the fruits of a one-way debate, relentlessly hammering CBS for "setting up" the vice president.

Instead of defending ourselves against attacks from politicians, the news media reports the attacks to viewers, readers and listeners who naturally believe the criticism because they seldom get the other side. How could the public avoid believing criticism that is objectively delivered without complaint from those being attacked?

The result is a level of public distrust that goes well beyond where it should be. The bias that exists in today's journalism does not justify the public's cynicism. The politicians who "run against the media" provide the extra measure of media bashing that inflames public anger.

The news media earned a whipping, for sure. Disingenuous and superficial news coverage is everywhere—on television, on radio, and even in the best newspapers. Biased, sometimes fraudulent reporting is not the rare exception it should be.

But on its worst days, a free and fair press is our only real chance at getting the truth.

The news media exists to try to tell you what "is" really "is." Politicians often try to define it as something that is far from the real truth.

Perhaps like no time in our history, today's politicians have the advantage in defining truth.

Armies of press aides, pseudojournalists and well-funded advocacy groups, are in place as an alternative to the traditional news media. The great irony is that the rise of this propaganda machine feeds on the belief that the news media is biased. Yet often there is no one more biased than those who hurl the charge.

If the press is not believed largely because politicians and their allies turned Americans against it, then the press is not free but under the thumb of politicians. And without a free press, there is no democracy.

3

A President Lies

It is the day a president lies.[1]

It is 10:37 A.M. Eastern Standard Time on January 26, 1998. President Bill Clinton begins to speak in the Roosevelt Room of the White house, a windowless conference room steps away from the Oval Office.

The president picked a grand room for this lie. Its rich history and formal style lend an air of credibility. Such an official setting will make this lie seem more believable. After all, how could the president of the United States stand in such a place and break faith with the American people?

The Roosevelt Room originally served as the presidential office when the West Wing was built in 1902. Today it is the private conference room for presidents and their top advisers. It is an inner sanctum for the most powerful job on Earth.

The room bears the personal touch of several presidents. Franklin Roosevelt, who relocated the presidential office to the Oval Office in 1934, kept an aquarium and fishing mementos here. He called it the Fish Room. John Kennedy mounted a sailfish that he caught in Acapulco, Mexico. President Nixon named the room in 1969 to honor Theodore Roosevelt for building the West Wing and Franklin Roosevelt for expanding it.

Clinton stands in front of a portrait of former President Theodore Roosevelt above the fireplace. It shows the famously energetic president in uniform and on horseback as commander of the Rough Riders in the Spanish-American War. These next few months will be a rough ride for the country.

Teddy Roosevelt is the one who dubbed the presidency a "bully pulpit." Clinton is at the pulpit today.

Reporters ushered into the room were told the president would take no questions. Several Clinton administration officials are on hand. Vice President Al Gore is here. First Lady Hillary Clinton is in the room.

The president was not scheduled to be here. Officially, this is an unveiling of a $2 billion child care after-school program.[2]

But the headlines of the morning newspapers show the real purpose of this gathering, revealing exactly why Clinton is here:

"A crisis with no parallel"—*Washington Post*

"White House acts to contain furor as concern grows"—*New York Times*

"Clinton fights to save his presidency"—*Chicago Tribune*

"Ex-intern accused of tryst with president"—*Los Angeles Times*

Five days earlier, the rumor mill went public. The name Monica S. Lewinsky first surfaced in major newspapers, shortly after popping up on the Internet. The newspapers reported that the twenty-four-year-old former White House intern was being questioned by prosecutors about allegations that she and Clinton had an affair and that he encouraged her to lie under oath in a civil lawsuit deposition.

PARSE THAT SENTENCE

The White House was under siege. Clinton's remarks in the first days after the story broke only led to more questions. He told PBS anchor Jim

Lehrer that there was no "improper relationship." Pressed for an explanation, he said, "There is no sexual relationship."

Why had the president limited this remark to the present tense? reporters asked White House aides. They were well schooled in paying close attention to Clinton's words. He had a history of carefully choosing words with a literal meaning that could be quite different from the impression he wished to give. The technical meaning of Clinton's phrasing—"there is no sexual relationship"—was as limited as it could be. He was saying only that he wasn't in a relationship at the time of the interview, which was true.

The press room at the White House buzzed with varying interpretations of the president's limited denial. He had not stemmed the tide. The pressure was on. Reporters hounded Clinton's staff all day. When would he directly address the American people about it?

It is a cycle we often see at the White House. Presidents struggle to avoid commenting on things they don't want to talk about. Usually, they get away with it. This was not one of those times. Clinton caved to the clamor for more presidential words, but it would be an intensely orchestrated moment, and he was not about to let reporters pepper him with questions.

As Clinton began to speak in the Roosevelt Room on January 26, he had already seen the polls. They were not good. A *Washington Post* poll just published showed that 57 percent of the Americans surveyed thought Clinton did indeed have the affair with an intern, and 36 percent thought he should resign because of it.

Even Clinton's political friends and many of his advisers were doubting him.

The president's defenders on television talk shows were struggling in vain to explain his actions.

White House aides Paul Begala and Rahm Emanuel, along with political consultant James Carville, appeared on several shows in the days leading up to Clinton's appearance in the Roosevelt Room. They declared that they believed Clinton and asked the public to withhold judgment. But they could not answer a simple question: If he did not have an affair with Lewinsky, what was his relationship with her? Why did he reportedly give her a dress and other personal gifts?

A roaring debate within the White House ensued. Should he step forward, admit the relationship, and ask forgiveness? Pollsters advised that it was too soon, that the public needed more time to get used to the idea. His lawyers vehemently argued against the contrition strategy. They feared that independent prosecutor Kenneth Starr would pounce, perhaps even file criminal charges against the president.

Clinton's advisers found it excruciatingly difficult to guide the president because they did not know the truth. Only he and perhaps one or two of his lawyers knew what really happened with Lewinsky.

They were not even sure exactly what he was about to say in the Roosevelt Room as news cameras prepared to broadcast his remarks live to the nation.

CHOOSING TO LIE

In the end, what Clinton said about Lewinsky took only twenty seconds and sixty-two words. And he had chosen to lie.

But first he pretended to be on hand to talk about child care. This was a calculated maneuver often deployed by politicians seeking to blame the media. When they finally answer media inquiries they would rather avoid, they often stage the moment in a context that potentially makes the media look out of sync with the public.

Clinton wanted Americans to get this message: Here is our president trying to do something good for kids, but those ridiculous reporters only want to talk about his sex life.

He did his best to underscore that message at the top of his remarks.

"Tomorrow, in the State of the Union address, I will spell out what we seek to do on behalf of our children to prepare them for the twenty-first century," Clinton said after greeting his wife, the vice president, his education secretary, several senators, and other dignitaries in the room. He ignored the assembled reporters.[3]

Never mind that Clinton had not even been scheduled to appear at this event until he decided to talk publicly about his sex life. He was not here because he wanted to talk about kids, or he would have planned to do so in the first place.

But in his next 688 words, Clinton only talked grandly about education policy. They could be the most forgettable words in the history of presidential speech making in the Roosevelt Room.

"In six minutes of policy talk, Clinton folded his hands, stuffed them in his suit pockets, gripped the podium, and rifled the pages of his speech," Sandra Sobieraj of the Associated Press wrote in a wire report distributed later in the day. "Twice he paused and licked his lips. He glanced left, right and down, but not once did he make eye contact with the reporters or camera lenses watching intently from the back of the room."[4]

Then he spoke the fateful words.

"I want to say one thing to the American people. I want you to listen to me. . . . I did not have sexual relations with that woman, Miss Lewinsky. I never told anybody to lie, not a single time—never. These allegations are false. And I need to go back to work for the American people."

THAT OTHER WEST WING AFFAIR

It was not the first time in recent years that the West Wing set the scene for a president facing charges of marital infidelity.[5]

President George H. W. Bush invoked the majesty of this venue to bat away a question about his personal life.

On August 11, 1992, Bush sat down in the Oval Office for an interview with NBC *Dateline* cohost Stone Phillips. The president was in the fight of his life, struggling for reelection against Democrat Bill Clinton. For months, the Bush campaign had delighted in the frenzied media coverage of stories of Clinton's infidelities.

Ten days before Bush's NBC interview, the Bush campaign had tried to revive wavering press interest in Clinton's personal life. Bush adviser Mary Matalin sent a memorandum to the campaign press corps noting that Clinton had hired investigators to deal with "bimbo eruptions." The charge was true, and the phrase "bimbo eruptions" was one that a Clinton aide had once used.

But the effect of the Matalin memo was not what the Bush team intended. Rather than renewing the news media's interest in Clinton's infidelities, the press began asking questions about a long-standing rumor that her boss once had an affair. Reporters decided that if the Bush campaign was going to raise Clinton's personal life in an official campaign document, then it was fair game to delve into stories about Bush's past.

NBC's Phillips wasted little time in asking the question while he and Bush sat in the Oval Office for the nationally broadcast interview.

Phillips: "Have you ever had an affair?"

Bush: "I'm not going to take any sleaze questions. I gave you a little warning. You see, you're perpetuating the sleaze by even asking the question, to say nothing of asking it in the Oval Office."

It does not take a careful reader to notice that Bush did not answer the question. Instead, he blamed the questioner for raising such an inappropriate topic in the majestic setting of the Oval Office.

Earlier that day, Bush was forced to deny specific allegations published in the morning edition of the *New York Post*. During a press conference at his vacation home in Maine, Bush was asked about the reports of an affair in 1984.

"It's a lie," Bush said, in answer to the question posed by CNN's Mary Tillotson. His press secretary, Marlin Fitzwater, was furious at the reporter. He later threatened that she "will never work around the White House again."

But Phillips was going further with his question in the White House. He wasn't limiting the scope to a specific allegation. He was broadly asking if Bush had ever had an affair.

Bush's response is a classic example of shifting blame to the questioner and making the reporter's disrespect the issue. Throughout the exchange, he never answers the question that his own campaign team had been so eager for reporters to pursue against his opponent.

> Phillips: The nature and character of this year's campaign has been that allegations about the candidates' private lives have been in the air. How did we get to this point?
>
> Bush: I don't know, I don't know. And it's not pleasant, it's ugly to go after your family and children. But it hasn't happened before this campaign. I've been through quite a few, and I don't know what it is. But it's ugly and I don't want any part of it. And I think the media needs a little discipline on this, to be very honest with you.
>
> Phillips: Governor Clinton has been asked directly . . .
>
> Bush: Be careful now, because this interview might end.
>
> Phillips: So let me ask you. Have you ever had an affair?
>
> Bush: I'm not going to take any sleaze questions. I gave you a little warning. You see, you're perpetuating the sleaze by even asking the question, to say nothing of asking it in the Oval Office, and I don't think you ought to do that and I'm not going to answer the question.
>
> Phillips: You were asked this morning to respond to a very specific allegation which you very strongly denied, and I was just asking a more general question because I think it goes to the point of character . . .
>
> Bush: And I've just given you the answer. I've just answered the question for you. That's it.
>
> Phillips: Isn't a reference to "bimbo explosions" by one of your staff people taking the low road?
>
> Bush: Is it any worse than what you've asked about today? Is it? Do you have any basis to accuse me by inference of anything?

Phillips: I didn't accuse you of anything.

Bush: No, you didn't, but you're perpetuating it—and that's the problem with the sleaze business. What happened there, they were quoting the words of the Clinton campaign person. And I didn't like it, and I said don't do it again, because it does perpetuate sleaze. And I made it very clear I didn't like that. And then here you come into this office, just without accusing me of anything, but just the very questioning like that perpetuates the very thing that then you go out and say, reporters, oh, we don't want anything to do with this, we don't like it. Do you see my point at all?

Phillips: Well, I do take your point, and the question may not be one of vital interest to the country, but it is . . .

Bush: It's what they call prurient interest.

Phillips: But the issue of character has been raised in this campaign, even by your own people. And without going to the specifics of the reports that came out this morning, it seems fair to ask you in a general sense the question.

Bush: I don't think it's fair; I think it perpetuates sleaze. And I didn't like it when reference was made to a quote by the campaign manager of Clinton. The quote was, as I understand it, using those very words. But I thought by inference that looked like we were in the sleaze business, and I said don't do it. And then suddenly, after years in public service and a very happy marriage, I am hit by a wave of questions like yours sitting here today. And I should think you'd be a little ashamed of yourself, because it just is beneath—you don't intend it this way, but it just drags down the political process. That's why I've told you that's all I'm going to say about it.

Bush dodged the question, and his protest at its inappropriateness rings a bit hollow given that his campaign supporters were fanning those very flames against his opponent.

But at least he did not lie.

"I DID NOT HAVE SEXUAL RELATIONS . . . "

Less than four years after Bush dodged a question about his sex life, Clinton chose a different path. He stood up in the White House and told one of the biggest whoppers in presidential history.

When finished, he fixed a "lingering glower on reporters," according to Sandra Sobieraj of the Associated Press, and walked out of the Roosevelt Room. It was 10:44 A.M. Eastern Standard Time.[6]

The sentence that most reverberates is the one that turned out most clearly to be a lie: "I did not have sexual relations with that woman, Miss Lewinsky."

Could there be a lower moment in presidential history? It was a pitiful story handled with utter disregard for a president's obligation to tell the truth to the American people.

There were pathetic attempts to parse Clinton's words in ways that made them accurate. Technically, sexual relations means intercourse, and the president did not have intercourse with this woman, we were told.

But on the day the president spoke these words, the message was clear. He was denying any sexual activity with Lewinsky.

Two and half hours later, White House Press Secretary Michael McCurry fielded news media questions in the West Wing briefing room. It too was aired live on national television.

As McCurry settled into the podium for what he knew would be a stormy session with reporters, he tried to muster his trademark wit to make the best of the situation.

"Why do I get the feeling there's like millions of people looking at their television sets saying, Why are they interrupting my soaps for this guy who never says anything?" he wondered. "Anybody got an answer to that?"[7]

"You're so photogenic," one reporter offered.

When the discussion turned to the president's remarks, it was clear that McCurry had no interest in explaining exactly what Clinton meant.

He dodged a question about the meaning of Clinton's words that he had no "sexual relations" with Lewinsky.

"I think the president was very straightforward in his comment, and I'm not going to dignify the question," McCurry answered. "I think every American that heard him knows exactly what he meant with the question. He didn't leave any ambiguity in it whatsoever."

Asked again if Clinton meant he had no sexual encounter whatsoever with the woman, McCurry said nothing more and called on another reporter for another question.

Faced with what many believed to be a brazen presidential lie, the news media was at a loss. A mountain of circumstantial evidence belied Clinton's passionate denial.

Most of the next-day newspaper accounts struggled to capture the unprecedented drama of the occasion while trying to sort through the meaning of the president's words.

"A defiant President Clinton wagged his finger at the cameras and thumped the lectern Monday as he insisted he did not have sex with a young White House intern or ask her to deny it under oath," the *Chicago Tribune*'s Roger Simon wrote in the newspaper's January 27 edition.[8]

"An angry President Clinton yesterday emphatically denied that he had 'sexual relations' with a young White House intern," the *Washington Times*' Paul Bedard wrote.[9]

Bedard showed a bit more skepticism than Simon, choosing to put the sexual relations phrase in quotes. The more cautious handling allowed Bedard to stop short of reporting the impression that Clinton wanted to give, that he had not had sex at all with Lewinsky. Clinton was famous for leaving impressions that did not necessarily match his exact choice of words, thus offering him an escape route if he needed it later on.

In Simon's lead paragraph, on the other hand, he reported that Clinton insisted "he did not have sex." For the moment, that is what

Clinton wanted to communicate. But he had hoped to later parse the remark by saying he was speaking only of sexual intercourse.[10]

Many reporters were stunned by the sheer emotion of Clinton's remarks. Was he acting, or was this the genuine indignation of a president who had been unfairly accused?

As Jim Nolan of the *Philadelphia Daily News* wrote, "We heard what he said, but do we know what he meant?"

Nolan nailed the basic dilemma reporters faced in handling Clinton's comments, which his press secretary had done nothing to clarify.

"Depending on whom you ask," Nolan wrote, "the embattled chief executive yesterday either set the record straight with a blanket denial of an affair with former White House intern Monica Lewinsky, or he bent it a little to get cover from a flowering sex scandal that could kill his presidency."[11]

There was such confusion about the Clinton denial that the *New York Post* reached out to body language experts for help. But alas, even those sources were in conflict.

"Body-language experts clashed on whether his outrage came from conviction or coaching," the *New York Post* reported.[12]

The president's personal popularity with the American people was another factor giving the news media pause on this story. If reporters jumped too hard, would this become just another case of a popular politician turning the public against the news media?

Despite the public's growing belief that Clinton committed adultery, in this case and others, he maintained approval ratings near 60 percent.

Yet if the news media seemed to be protecting Clinton, they would again face the charges of liberal bias. The balancing act was plain to see. Most news organizations gave the story big play, which pleased Clinton's detractors, but they gave it the spin that the White House wanted. Clinton's team wanted him to be seen as genuinely outraged, which served to make his denial more believable.

Television reports of Clinton's denial focused even more intensely on the president's emotions.

ABC's Sam Donaldson, who had tried to shout questions to Clinton as he left the room, reported on the network's evening newscast that the president gave "an emotional and somewhat angry statement."

CBS's Dan Rather noted that that "the president speaks forcefully with his most emphatic denial yet of sex and lies in the Monica Lewinsky case."

NBC's Tom Brokaw introduced the network's coverage by saying, "An angry President Clinton fights back."

There was something for everyone in this coverage. Clinton was on the ropes, but he was fighting back. With his reputation as the "Comeback Kid" for rising above difficulties, the dynamics were in place for another Clinton rally.

The upshot of Clinton's denial was that he bought time. Most important for the White House, the gossip about an impending presidential resignation faded away. Clinton weathered the moment. The public accepted his words, so energetically delivered, largely because the news media did not challenge the president's truthfulness as forcefully as the situation required.

ABC's Peter Jennings summed up the president's denial in the most forgiving way imaginable, although hinting at the potential wiggle room in Clinton's words.

"I think, to many people, it was reassuring," Jennings told his viewers moments after Clinton's remarks. "He couldn't have been more definitive, as far as the look on his face, his tone of voice, the way he expressed himself—as long as the word 'relationship' covers everything."

There was enough on the record by this time to seriously question the truthfulness of Clinton's denial. Lengthy tapes of Lewinsky describing their sexual relations were circulating. The president himself had recently met with her. Her lawyers had reached agreement with prosecutors to let her testify in exchange for immunity.

And there was plenty to suggest that Clinton was being clever in his choice of words, "sexual relations." It was not just his personal history of word parsing that should have tipped off the press corps. On one of the Lewinsky phone tapes, she said he had told her that oral sex did not count as a sexual relationship.

It was all so unseemly that many in the news media just wanted the story to go away, and many hoped Clinton's denial would make it go away—even if they did not believe him.

Armed with polls showing the public to be taking the story in stride, many newsroom bosses hoped the story had run its course.

But even if the public does not care about sexual misdeeds in the White House, the media cannot back off when the president of the United States stands up in the West Wing and lies to the American people—even if he is "just lying about sex," an excuse often cited to dismiss the story.

If there are any standards left for presidential behavior, surely this crossed the line.

But as time passed and a Senate impeachment trial came and went, Clinton weathered it all. The narrative of this story in the news coverage ultimately became what the White House wanted it to be, nothing more than a tale of political partisanship.

In the end, the Lewinsky affair was covered as a struggle for political power between Republicans and Democrats. And that is how it came to be seen by the public.

After Clinton won the Senate impeachment trial on February 12, 1999, public opinion turned against the Republicans, whose leaders in Congress posted their lowest poll ratings in years.

Lost in the coverage of the episode as political warfare was the unforgivable act of a president using his office and the news media to appear on camera before the American people, essentially looking them in the eye and telling them a miserable lie.

If the news media exists for anything, it should be to call the foul loudly when presidents misbehave so badly.

4

Spinning Lies

Lying is an art form in Washington. The pros call it spin. A better word for spin is what we used to call it: propaganda.

What is a lie? I have a simple definition. It is the product of any intent to deceive.

The trouble with holding yourself to this standard is that you will often catch yourself in a lie. If any intent to deceive is a lie, then there is a lot of lying in our world.

But it is better to have a broad definition for lying, even if it means you often violate your own standard, than to water down the definition so that you can tell yourself that you never lie.

That is what happens in Washington. The consensus definition of lying is so narrowly drawn that bald-faced lies become truth. And the news media plays along, preferring less provocative words like "spin" for what are basically lies.

In Washington, we follow Mark Twain's maxim: "Truth is the most valuable thing we have. Let us economize it."[1] Sometimes, spin really is something less than a lie. But even if the precise words are truthful, the spinner's intent to deceive makes it a lie.

Deceitfully spinning the truth is so common and expected in Washington that politicians often go off the record when they want to tell a reporter the truth. What does that tell you?

Twisting the truth has gotten so perverse in Washington that few believe a quote if it is said in public. But if it is said off the record as an anonymous quote, it rings true.

The news media is far too forgiving of politicians who want to tell the real truth anonymously. Reporters are suckers for this technique because it makes their reports seem more exotic. Sometimes, like with a quote from a Clinton cabinet member later in this chapter, we have no choice. It is the only way to get the information out.

Politicians lie because we reward them for it. When first accused of having an affair with a young intern, President Bill Clinton did something considered a terrible mistake. He lied. Although a moral lapse, it was not a political mistake.

Although Clinton's original lie caused him a world of legal trouble, it also saved his presidency from a quick death. It gave him cover while he waited for the public to get used to the truth about his scandalous White House affair.

Politicians often lie because we don't want to hear the truth. Their view recalls the words of Jack Nicholson's character Colonel Nathan R. Jessup in the courtroom thriller *A Few Good Men*. Accused of giving an order that leads to a Marine's death, Nicholson defends his actions as a necessary evil. When the prosecutor, played by Tom Cruise, says, "I want the truth," Nicholson's character famously responds, "You can't handle the truth."[2]

GAMBLING WITH THE TRUTH

Presidents who pay attention to history find that telling the truth got their predecessors into trouble. President Jimmy Carter once blundered badly by telling the truth as he saw it.

On the night of July 15, 1979, after ten days of closed-door meetings at Camp David with leaders from throughout the country, President Carter delivered what became known as his "Malaise Speech." The national was facing many troubles. A gas shortage, the result of manipulation by foreign oil producers, produced long lines at the pump. Inflation was on the rise. And the public was as cynical about their government as ever.

Although the word "malaise" was not in Carter's text, it became the emblem on his unusually candid description of how he viewed the emotional condition of the country. His nationally broadcast speech that night is one of the most remarkable in presidential history. No president before or since Carter talked directly to the American people in quite this way:

> I want to speak to you tonight about . . . a fundamental threat to American democracy. . . . The threat is nearly invisible in ordinary ways. It is a crisis of confidence. It is a crisis that strikes at the very heart and soul and spirit of our national will. We can see this crisis in the growing doubt about the meaning of our own lives and in the loss of a unity of purpose for our nation. . . . Our people are losing faith, not only in government itself but in the ability as citizens to serve as the ultimate rulers and shapers of our democracy. . . . Human identity is no longer defined by what one does, but by what one owns. . . . The symptoms of this crisis of the American spirit are all around us. . . . Two-thirds of our people do not even vote. The productivity of American workers is actually dropping, and the willingness of Americans to save for the future has fallen below that of all other people in the Western world. . . . The gap between our citizens and our government has never been so wide. The people are looking for honest answers, clear leadership, not false claims and evasiveness and politics as usual. We must face the truth, and then we can change our course. We simply must have faith in each other, faith in our ability to govern ourselves, and faith in the future of this nation.[3]

Carter gambled with the truth and lost. Instead of getting credit for leveling with the public, he was blamed for causing the malaise he described. It haunts him still.

During the 2004 presidential campaign, Vice President Dick Cheney warned that Democratic nominee John Kerry would return the nation to the "malaise" of the Carter era.

The American people could not handle Carter's truth. They voted him out of office. For once, a president tried to be blunt. Not only did he say that things were not as rosy as most presidents pretend, but he was saying that the American people bore some responsibility. It is heresy for a president to tell Americans that they are less than perfect. Yet here was Carter on national television telling them that they were in a foul mood and that they should do something about it. He was saying that it was up to the American people to take charge of their plight and get in gear.

Given what happened to Carter a year later when he was run out of office by the perpetually upbeat Ronald Reagan, it is unlikely we will ever see a president be so candid again.

But Carter's vice president, Walter Mondale, did not learn the lesson so well demonstrated by his former boss. When running for the presidency himself, Mondale told the truth about taxes in his acceptance speech for the Democratic nomination in 1984. He said he planned to raise taxes in order to cut the mounting deficit in the federal budget.

"Running as a tax raiser, that was a brilliant political move," said University of Virginia political scientist Larry Sabato.[4]

Never again would a serious candidate for the presidency come clean with plans to raise taxes, even though some went on to do so after getting elected. Two presidents who came after the "Mondale Moment," as it became known, did raise taxes despite campaigning against doing so: George H. W. Bush and Bill Clinton.

Bush was steadfast in his 1988 campaign, delivering the famous line, "Read my lips, no new taxes." As president, he agreed to higher taxes. In 1992, Clinton promised not to raise taxes "to pay for new programs." He later pushed the biggest tax increase in U.S. history through Congress, insisting that he had kept his campaign pledge because the higher taxes only paid for old programs. But there is no escaping that he intended voters in 1992 to believe that he would not raise taxes at all.

Had Bush or Clinton told the whole truth during their campaigns, they might not have been elected. Indeed, Bush's reversal of his 1988 tax pledge was a major contributing factor in his reelection defeat four years later.

"For many of us, telling the truth is a moment of strength," Sabato said. "But for politicians, it can be a moment of weakness."

THE REWARDS OF LYING

Today, politicians take few chances in telling the truth, never daring to tell the public anything it does not want to hear.

In lying to the American people about his affair, Clinton concluded that they could not handle the truth. And he could not handle the consequences of the truth, at least not until his lawyers and advisers could come up with a survival strategy.

My guess is that many Americans, including some in the news media, wanted Clinton to lie because they just did not want to hear any more of the sordid details. Instead, things just got worse.

Clinton's cabinet topped the list of those who wanted the Monica story to go away. Just a few days before the president lied to the nation about his affair, he lied to his cabinet about it.

One who was there told me they were relieved when the president denied the affair at their January 23, 1998, meeting in the Cabinet Room of the West Wing.

"I'll admit some suspicion that he was spinning us, but I blocked those feelings because I wanted to believe him," the Clinton cabinet member said.[5]

It was a stunning display of Clinton's commitment to this lie.

After denying that he had an affair with the White House intern, Clinton asked these loyal supporters to go repeat his claim to the news media.

Four of Clinton's most visible cabinet members agreed to talk to the phalanx of news cameras assembled outside the West Wing. Pointedly, two women took the lead: Secretary of State Madeleine Albright and Health and Human Services Secretary Donna Shalala.

"I believe that the allegations are completely untrue," Albright said as she stood with the other cabinet members on the pavement outside the official entrance to the West Wing.

"I'll second that, definitely," Commerce Secretary William Daley added. "Third it," Shalala said. Education Secretary Richard Riley, the fourth Clinton cabinet member going before cameras that day, echoed Daley's endorsement.

"I think what he thinks . . . I absolutely do," Riley said of the denial.[6]

It sounded as if Riley was saying he would believe the president no matter what he said.

Only if that were so. Surely the nation can believe the president's denial if he is willing to sit in the Cabinet Room and issue the denial to those who run his government.

Clinton gambled that the awe and respect for the trappings of his office would convince Americans he was telling the truth.

Now that we know Clinton was lying, it is so amazing to think that he would dispatch his secretary of state and other cabinet members out to spread his lie.

No matter that the substance of this story was so silly. Those who think that a president's sexual life should be separated from his job have a point. Who cares what he does if it does not affect his work?

That was the mantra among the press corps during Kennedy's term in office. Reporters on the White House beat knew that he was unfaithful, but to this day many defend the silence of the press corps on the grounds that it had nothing to do with his official work.

But even if you accept that view, Clinton crossed a line. Once the sexual allegations were publicly made, he chose to abuse the public's respect for his office. The historic rooms and images of the White House served as the backdrop for his big lie. Officials of his government on the White House steps reinforced this orchestration of presidential accessories to make us believe him.

This is what the dictionaries call propaganda—deceptive or distorted information that is systematically spread. The key to defining propaganda is that it be "systematically spread," usually by a government or an institution.[7]

THE HISTORY OF PROPAGANDA

The use of propaganda has been around since the beginning of recorded time. The word "propaganda" is a Latin term first coined by the Catholic Church in 1622. Pope Gregory XV formed the Sacred Congregation for the Propagation of the Faith, a committee of cardinals that still exists today for spreading Catholicism to new countries. The Latin title was *congregation de propaganda fide*.[8]

Paintings, sculpture, and architecture became tools for spreading the word of God in the hands of these seventeenth-century Catholic leaders. Their propaganda was meant to deliver religious hope.

Propaganda did not gain its sinister meaning until the two world wars, especially in Adolf Hitler's Germany.

Recognizing the word's negative connotations, Pope John Paul II changed the congregation's name in 1982. It is now called the Congregation for the Evangelization of Peoples.

Until Hitler, propaganda was considered a good thing, an acceptable way for governments to rally the people. During World War I, the United States and Britain proudly distributed what officials called propaganda posters designed to generate support for the first war against Germany.

Hitler forever changed the image of propaganda. He used the public rallying techniques of democracies and Christian evangelism for evil. Joseph Goebbels, his official minister of propaganda, perfected the use of the news media, film, theater, literature, music, and fine arts to present a positive image of the Nazi Party.[9]

Scenes of Nazi propaganda influenced a generation of Americans to see evil in the ways of promoting a government's agenda. But government's dependence on propaganda did not go away.

Modern propagandists have a new, more benign-sounding term for what they do.

Today we call it spin. We laugh about it. The news media teases political aides for "spinning" the news to put their bosses in the best light.

We should go back to calling it propaganda. And the American people should keep alert to signs of propaganda from our politicians. Some of it is benign, perhaps in service to a good cause.

But deception in the pursuit of a good cause only encourages the deceiver to go further.

SPINNING THE DRUG WAR

President George H. W. Bush might have gone too far in a phenomenal episode of the so-called Drug War.[10]

On September 5, 1989, Bush spoke to the nation from the Oval Office, holding up a plastic bag filled with a white chunky substance.

"This is crack cocaine," Bush sternly announced. He said it was "seized a few days ago in a park across the street from the White House. . . . It could easily have been heroin or PCP."

The prop was meant to show how pervasive the drug culture had become. Illegal drugs were being sold at the doorstep of the White House!

But it turned out to be a setup. Agents of the Drug Enforcement Administration (DEA) had struggled to lure a drug dealer to nearby Lafayette Park for the sole purpose of creating a dramatic prop for the president's speech.

Indeed, a DEA agent later told the *Washington Post* that the agency faced considerable difficulty in obtaining the crack to match the words of Bush's speechwriters. Four days before the speech was given, an undercover DEA agent posing as a drug buyer persuaded an eighteen-year-old drug dealer to meet him at the park across the street from the White House.

"Where the [expletive] is the White House?" the high school senior replied in a conversation that was secretly tape-recorded by the DEA. When told it was the residence of the president, he replied, "Oh, you mean where Reagan lives." The dealer found his way to Lafayette Park, and the president's prop was secured.

"We had to manipulate him to get him down there," DEA agent William McMullan told the *Post*. "It wasn't easy."

The DEA agent paid $2,400 for three ounces of crack later delivered to the West Wing.

A few days later, when the ruse became public, Bush defended what his staff and the DEA had done.

"I think it was great because it sent a message to the United States that even across from the White House they can sell drugs," Bush said. "Every time that some guy gets caught selling drugs, he pleads that somebody is luring [him] someplace."

Critics thought otherwise. Senator John Breaux, a Louisiana Democrat, thought the "staged" prop undermined the serious purpose of fighting illegal drugs.

"Is this really a drug war or is this theatrics and screenplay?" Breaux asked. "We don't need the president to lure drug pushers to Lafayette Park for photo opportunities."

Bush's son would later face similar criticism but in a much more grave context. Questions still persist about the legitimacy of President

George W. Bush's "evidence" that Iraqi dictator Saddam Hussein possessed weapons of mass destruction. Those claims helped justify the 2003 invasion of Iraq, but long after the first phase of combat had ended, the second Bush administration finally acknowledged they never did have the proof they had claimed. By then, 140,000 U.S. troops were stuck in Iraq with no dignified way out.

Spinning the evidence for war, whether it is a domestic drug war or a foreign invasion, is not something to be taken lightly. Yet, as a rule, spinning is a big joke to those in power and to many in the news media who report it.

THE SPIN ROOM

The presidential campaign debates made spin an institution. They feature a "spin room" for reporters to faithfully collect the postdebate propaganda.

The Commission on Presidential Debates, a group led by members of both political parties, takes care to set up the spin room. This is where aides and supporters of the candidates come to tell the news media how well their bosses did.

The spin starts even before presidential debates begin. Aides distribute press releases to the media called "pre-spin."

A candidate's team huddles before entering the spin room to devise uniform talking points for their coming interviews with the news media. The most careful attention is paid to crafting entertaining "sound bites" delivered to television outlets that depend on these attention-getting ploys to keep their viewers watching. If the boss did not really do so well, they must argue otherwise or risk demoralizing the candidate's supporters.

The spin room at presidential debates observes the rules that Hilter's propaganda chief deployed. Any student of Goebbels's methods can quickly discern his basic rules:

Propaganda must be centralized, planned, and executed by a single authority.

To get attention, propaganda is best distributed through an entertaining communications medium.

Propaganda must be carefully timed for maximum effect.

Propaganda is a tool of social control, designed to comfort the public in times of stress.

The time has come to call political spin what it is: propaganda. The word's sinister history should not scare the news media away from its use when appropriate. It is worse to let the propagandists get away with changing the name for what they do to a friendly-sounding word.

Reporting the truth in politics is a tricky enough business without letting politicians dummy down the nomenclature for their propaganda.

And politicians are getting better and better at spinning lies into what sounds like truth. It doesn't help that many politicians are lawyers.

Tinkering with the meaning of words is a lawyer's stock-in-trade. A lie isn't a lie unless the precise meaning of the words makes it a lie.

In political campaigns, the line between truth and lies is horribly blurred beyond all recognition, especially in television ads.

An avalanche of misinformation from both sides of the political aisle marked the closing days of the 2004 presidential election.

One of John Kerry's last television ads, labeled "The Truth About Taxes," was a lie.

"After nearly four years under George Bush, the middle class is paying the bigger share of America's tax burden and the wealthiest are paying less," the ad's narrator says.[11]

This ad is a good example of how facts that are literally true can be made into a lie.

It is technically true that the overall share of the tax burden went up by two-tenths of 1 percent for the middle 20 percent of earners under Bush's tax changes. But the ad clearly intends to leave the impression that the wealthy pay a smaller share than middle-income earners.

That is false. At the time of this ad, the most affluent 20 percent of taxpayers paid 63 percent of all U.S. taxes, according to the nonpartisan Tax Policy Center. Those in the middle 20 percent paid 10.5 percent, a much smaller share.

The Kerry ad was most careful to refer to the "share" of the tax burden. That's because all income groups actually paid less taxes as a result of Bush's cuts. Only the percentage share of the burden went up slightly for the middle-income group.

But anyone seeing this ad during the normal routine of life would clearly get the impression that middle-income Americans are paying more taxes than the wealthy. That impression would be a lie.

The Bush campaign was no slacker in the contest of deceitful ads.

The Annenberg Political Fact Check, a nonpartisan watchdog for campaign ads based at the University of Pennsylvania, reached a sad conclusion after monitoring all the 2004 ads.

"Both sides are making false or misleading claims in their ads," the Annenberg fact-checkers reported in the closing days of the campaign.[12]

Twisting an opponent's words is a time-honored technique that the Bush campaign deployed quite successfully.

A Bush closing-days ad began with this line: "John Kerry says we have to get back to the place where terrorists are a nuisance, like gambling and prostitution."

The ad refers to a *New York Times Magazine* interview of Kerry, published October 10, 2004. When asked what it would take to make Americans feel safe again, Kerry said,

> We have to get back to the place we were, where terrorists are not the focus of our lives, but they're a nuisance. . . . As a former law-enforcement person, I know we're never going to end prostitution. We're never going to end illegal gambling. But we're going to re-

duce it, organized crime, to a level where it isn't on the rise. It isn't threatening people's lives every day, and fundamentally, it's something that you continue to fight, but it's not threatening the fabric of your life.

Note that Kerry was responding to a question asking what it would take to make Americans feel safe again. Take the answer out of that context, as the Bush ad did, and it might sound as if he were saying terrorists are just a nuisance.

The next line of the announcer's text in the Bush ad hammers home its false premise: "Terrorists a nuisance?" And then it goes on to counter the false premise that Kerry dismissed the seriousness of the terrorist threat. Scrutinizing the text of these two ads shows just how difficult it is for the news media to give the truth a chance against such clever manipulations.

Most newspapers and television news outlets run truth-squad features, designed to show voters how some ads deceive them. But these efforts pale in comparison to how many people are exposed to the ads.[13]

The Bush and Kerry ads I've described ran about 10,000 times over seven days in forty-five cities. There is little that any news organization can do to reach that level of saturation.

And the media's credibility is at such a low point that politicians find a receptive audience for belittling sincere efforts to play watchdog.

When confronted about his ads during the 2004 campaign debates, President Bush did what comes naturally to politicians these days. He attacked the messenger. Democratic nominee John Kerry had just noted that "two leading national news networks" reported Bush had mischaracterized Kerry's health plan.

"With all due respect," Bush replied, "I'm not so sure it's credible to quote leading news organizations about—oh, never mind."[14]

The most difficult task for the news media is in drawing conclusions about which campaign in an election is lying the most.

One news chief's efforts to do so during the 2004 campaign got him into a world of trouble.

ABC Political Director Mark Halperin tried to give his campaign correspondents some direction in an internal memo that was leaked and widely distributed on the Internet.

"The current Bush attacks on Kerry involve distortions and taking things out of context in a way that goes beyond what Kerry has done," Halperin wrote to his staff. In a line that infuriated Bush sympathizers, he offered a suggestion on how to proceed.

Noting that "our responsibilities become quite grave" in the face of so much campaign distortion, Halperin wrote, "We have a responsibility to hold both sides accountable to the public interest, but that doesn't mean we reflexively and artificially hold both sides 'equally' accountable when the facts don't warrant that."

Halperin's memo concludes by echoing the sentiment of many in the news media at the end of the 2004 campaign:

> I'm sure many of you have this week felt the stepped up Bush efforts to complain about our coverage. This is all part of their efforts to get away with as much as possible with the stepped up, renewed efforts to win the election by destroying Senator Kerry at least partly through distortions. It's up to Kerry to defend himself, of course. But as one of the few news organizations with the skill and strength to help voters evaluate what the candidates are saying to serve the public interest, now is the time for all of us to step up and do that right.

Halperin was correct in these observations. The Bush campaign was much more effective at "destroying" their opponent "at least partly through distortions." Yet his memo, intended to be read only by his staff, is one of the few attempts by the news media to make this case.[15]

But saying so in a published or televised report obviously would be a lightning rod for attacks from those who are accused. This should not frighten reporters away from the task that Halperin described.

Just as it is for politicians, trying to be all things to all people is a slippery slope for the news media. Sometimes, fair and balanced reporting calls for an honest conclusion that might offend a political player.

So what. If it is an honestly drawn conclusion, well proven with the facts, let the offended side wail as much as they like.

At the end of the day, it is not the job of politicians to protect truth. They have an agenda. Often their agenda is a good thing for the country. And sometimes they deceive the public to prevent opponents from undermining that agenda.

But the news media must always seek truth. This doesn't always happen, but it doesn't mean that we shouldn't keep trying.

If the truth hurts or enrages our readers and viewers, we cannot back off. Reporters who lay off the truth or intend to deceive the public in any way no longer deserve the franchise. They should go into politics.

5

A War Story

It was a simple question, put to the White House press secretary on March 18, 2003, just days before the start of the Iraq War:

"Does it bother the president that most of the world is against this war?"[1]

Helen Thomas, who asked the question, did not become dean of the White House press corps by asking the easy ones, but she does try to keep it simple.

"Anybody at home watching this stuff would have asked such a question," Thomas said. "I thought it was important for the White House to explain why we were going to war. They were bragging in great detail about how we were going to drop bombs, but they didn't want to give clear answers about the reasons for war."[2]

Thomas's testy exchange with Ari Fleischer—just one of many in the weeks leading up to the Iraq War—began by simply asking if President George W. Bush cared that he was going into Iraq virtually alone, without a broad international coalition.

Instead of answering the question, Fleischer made Thomas the issue.

"Helen, this is an issue where you and I will never agree when you state your premise about what the people think," Fleischer said.

"This isn't you and I," Thomas responded. "This is a very legitimate question."

Fleischer then interrupted Thomas as she began citing public opinion polls detailing that half the American public opposed an immediate war in Iraq.

"I understand your strong opinions clearly. I'm not sure the American people agree with you," Fleischer said.[3]

Fleischer's handling of Thomas is typical of what has become a refined method for politicians facing tough questions from reporters. Make the reporters the issue by accusing them of bias.

Thomas had no illusions about what Fleischer was up to.

"It was all about demonizing the messenger," Thomas said. "By doing that, he knew the public would think, 'Why is she so unpatriotic? Why is she jeopardizing our troops?'"[4]

Although Thomas's opening question in the dialogue above delivered a punch—"most of the world is against this war"—there was considerable evidence at the time that she was correct, starting with recalcitrance at the UN Security Council.

It would have been easy for Fleischer to respond simply by disagreeing with Thomas's premise without asserting that she was just flacking her own personal opinions. But attacking the messenger is now ingrained in political rhetoric because it works. Politicians have so successfully persuaded Americans that reporters merely traffic their own bias that they need only make the charge and most people believe it.

The bullying of reporters has reached the point that many in the news media are afraid to challenge the powerful.

The Iraq War brought a new twist to the liberal tag on the news media. Many in the news business feared being labeled unpatriotic.

"Most news organizations were afraid of being branded 'anti-American,'" said one national television news anchor about the Iraq War. "The media establishment began to believe the label of 'liberal media' and, in the end, did a disservice to the American people by not asking the tough questions of our politicians and military leaders."[5]

A PRESS SUBDUED

The televised smack-downs between Ari Fleischer and Helen Thomas in the daily West Wing briefings became a staple of the lead-up to the Iraq War. They stood out because Thomas was one of only a handful of journalists with access to the White House who put tough questions to the Bush administration.

Indeed, the mainstream news coverage in the weeks before the Iraq War featured little from dissenters in Congress or elsewhere. Some cable news channel executives forbade those who opposed the war from appearing on their air.

"We were flatly told not to book anyone who opposed the war, even if they were U.S. senators," said a former producer for one of the cable news channels. Although no longer working for the channel, she is still employed in the television industry and asked not to be identified out of fear of reprisals.[6]

Only after the war—long afterward—did the news media get tough on the Bush administration, culminating in a testy April 13, 2004, presidential press conference where reporters repeatedly asked Bush if he should admit mistakes in his handling of the threat of terrorism against the United States.

Ironically, Bush did not call on the reporter who had asked the tough questions before the war—Helen Thomas. He was the first president to ignore Thomas at a prime-time press conference since she began working in the White House press corps during the Kennedy administration. Although she kept her front-row seat at daily briefings in the West Wing, the briefers seldom recognize her for a question when the TV cameras are rolling.

JEFFERSON AND LINCOLN AGAINST THE PRESS

The banishment of Helen Thomas is certainly not the first time that politicians tried to make annoying reporters go away. The Clinton White House routinely cut off access for those who most vigorously pursued the Lewinsky scandal.

Since the nation was founded, even our most cherished presidents have wanted to muzzle the press.

Thomas Jefferson hated the newspapers of his day. Some relentlessly pursued scandalous stories about his private life, including charges of a long-standing liaison between Jefferson and one of his slaves, Sally Hemings. Jefferson may have been the first American politician to dodge such a story by blaming the media. Genetic testing in 1998 showed a "strong likelihood" that Jefferson did father a child born to Hemings. The Thomas Jefferson Memorial Foundation issued a report in 2000 concluding that Jefferson had, in fact, fathered one or more of her children.

But in his day, Jefferson responded to the charges by attacking the press, offering a model for modern-day presidents facing similar claims.

"I deplore . . . the putrid state into which our newspapers have passed and the malignity, the vulgarity, and mendacious spirit of those who write for them," Jefferson wrote to a friend in 1814.[7]

Still, Jefferson was too proud of his role in founding a nation based on freedom of the press to take action against those who offended him.

"I know that I might have filled the courts of the United States with actions for these slanders and have ruined, perhaps, many persons who are not innocent," Jefferson wrote to a friend in Connecticut. "But this would be no equivalent for the loss of character. I leave them, therefore, to the reproof of their own consciences."[8]

Abraham Lincoln was less reserved when the press irritated him during the Civil War. At one point, he even sent troops to invade and shut down two newspapers in New York City. After the newspapers printed forged documents purporting to show that Lincoln would draft more New Yorkers for war duty, he wrote this chilling order to military authorities on May 18, 1864:

> Whereas, there has been wickedly and traitorously printed and published this morning, in the *"New York World"* and New York *"Journal of Commerce"* newspapers printed and published in the city of New York,—a false and spurious proclamation, purporting to be signed by the President, and to be countersigned by the Secretary of State, which publication is of a treasonable nature, designed to give aid and comfort to the enemies of the United States, and to the rebels now at war against the Government, and their aiders and abettors: you are therefore hereby commanded forthwith to arrest and imprison in any fort or military prison in your command, the editors, proprietors and publishers of the aforesaid newspapers, and all such persons as, after public notice has been given of the falsehood of said publication, print and publish the same, with intent to give aid and comfort to the enemy;—and you will hold the persons so arrested, in close custody, until they can be brought to trial before a military commission, for their offense. You will also take possession by military force, of the printing establishments of the *"New York World"* and *"Journal of Commerce,"* and hold the same until further order, and prevent any further publication therefrom.

The newspaper editors quickly apologized, saying they were duped by the forgery of the draft order. Lincoln released the jailed journalists, except for the two responsible for the hoax.[9]

There is an ominous relevance to Lincoln's actions against the press. Today, the government cites other suspensions of civil liberties by Lincoln as a precedent for detaining war prisoners. In times of war, it is argued, U.S. officials have the power to waive certain rights as Lincoln did.[10]

That same argument could someday be used to jail reporters as Lincoln did.

In times of peace or war, it is the nature of most politicians—in democracies or in dictatorships—to avoid scrutiny.

Politicians have devised many ways to mute the effects of an aggressive news media. And so often the news media itself is an unwitting partner. The demise of the daily White House press briefing is one example.

THE WHITE HOUSE BRIEFING AS PERFORMANCE ART

White House press briefings once were held out of public view, offering reporters a chance to explore complex issues with presidential aides. There was always a lot of give-and-take, but for the most part neither the reporters nor the White House staff used these West Wing briefings to score points with the public.

That all changed with the arrival of cable news channels and their need to fill seemingly endless hours of daily programming.

Bill Clinton's sexual scandal and the advent of cable news competition came roughly at the same time. Clinton's White House press secretary, Mike McCurry, became a daily fixture on television as he fielded some of the most awkward, personal, and unpleasant questions any presidential spokesperson ever had to face in the West Wing briefings.

But as happened with Fleischer's briefings before the Iraq War, the spotlight on reporters asking questions presented a positive result for the White House. The spectacle of nagging reporters repetitively asking rude and insensitive questions made martyrs of McCurry and Fleischer.

Seeing the raw process of reporters trying to wheedle information out of uncooperative bureaucrats tends to make many Americans feel sorry for the bureaucrats. This is because many Americans do not understand just how much these bureaucrats deceive us and how necessary it is sometimes to try to make them angry to get them off message.

In the Reagan White House, aides loved to have the president walk by a gaggle of reporters shouting questions at him—all in full view of the cameras. Americans saw what appeared to be horribly disrespectful reporters yelling at their leader. What they didn't know is how Reagan's staff had so limited access to him, forcing reporters to shout questions in those settings because that was about as close to him as they ever got.

As daily news reporters like Helen Thomas were shoved out of the picture, pundits stepped into their place. Reporters no longer stand in the shoes of average Americans to ask the questions and raise the issues that those in their living rooms have no opportunity to do.

Pundits now represent the public as reporters once did. But pundits are a different breed. They are opinion merchants. Like politicians, they represent constituencies. But they do serve a role.

Ann Coulter is a pundit. A conservative firebrand who rails against liberals and rallies like-minded supporters, she feeds a mass of devoted followers with columns, books, and television appearances.

Outrageous statements are a pundit's stock-in-trade. Coulter, for instance, once advocated war against Muslims, saying the United States "should invade their countries, kill their leaders and convert them to Christianity."[11]

Conservative pundits like Coulter were critical to maintaining the momentum for war as the Bush administration prepared to invade Iraq.

THE TV GENERALS

The invasion of Iraq brought the return of another type of pundit that has become a staple during wartime—the TV generals. Retired military officers emerged as a news media force during the Persian Gulf War, the first major military conflict since the advent of cable news.

The all-news channels found the TV generals to be quite popular with viewers. Their gruff, no-nonsense demeanor delights male viewers in particular. They come across like John Wayne, inspiring confidence in the U.S. military.

One of the TV generals, Wesley Clark, even used the platform of his punditry on CNN to run for the presidency in 2004.

Going back to the Persian Gulf War, those still running the military welcomed this trend. The TV generals could be relied on to echo the Pentagon's daily message. Media critics complained that they were military propagandists masquerading as independent news analysts.

But the early days of the Iraq War showcased another trait in these well-spoken military men. They can be very blunt. And they stunned the White House with their candor.

As the invasion of Iraq unfolded, the TV generals grew increasingly critical of Secretary of Defense Donald Rumsfeld's determination to occupy the nation quickly with fewer forces than conventional military strategists suggested were necessary. It turns out that the strategists overruled by Rumsfeld were griping behind the scenes to the TV generals.

While the civilian news media remained mostly clueless about this debate, the TV generals led the way in outing the strategic debate inside the Pentagon. Ironically, it took former military officials to do the job that professional journalists had failed to do.

In late March 2003, the U.S.-led forces in Iraq were bogged down. Things were not moving as quickly as the Pentagon had predicted. It was the first time that the Iraq War produced troubling news for the Bush administration. Until this point, the war appeared to be the unfettered victory march that the White House had hoped for.

Reporters embedded with the troops began relaying news of units stuck under fire, unable to proceed as rapidly as planned.

Military pundits on television began griping that this showed how underresourced the invasion had been.

"We are outgunned," retired U.S. Air Force Lieutenant General Michael Short bluntly told me shortly after making a similar comment on a cable news channel. The former commander of NATO air forces in the Bosnian war was among several military types hired by networks to be on-air consultants.[12]

Short was especially critical of Rumsfeld. He and other military pundits believed Rumsfeld had wrongly nixed Pentagon plans for more troops and armor in the battlefield before racing toward Baghdad.

The result, Short said, was "supply lines that were more at risk" in the first week as coalition forces got bogged down facing stiff resistance in southern Iraq.

Military pundits like Short were far more direct and pointed about such observations than most in the news media. Reporters embedded with troops faced severe restrictions on how much they could say about tactical matters.

In exchange for officially traveling with the troops, the news media had to agree to certain guidelines. Troop strength and deployments were at the top of the list of tactical issues these reporters had to avoid.

But the embedded reporters did provide vivid accounts and footage of troops under fire, severely hindered in their efforts to cover and occupy as much Iraqi ground as possible.

It was up to the military analysts hired by the news media to draw the bigger picture.

As it turned out, these military pundits were just about the only vocal critics. Even those politicians who opposed the war were being careful. They feared the Bush White House would attack them as unsupportive of the troops.

The Democratic presidential candidates, just gearing into the 2004 campaign, faced a difficult choice. Here was an opportunity to raise doubts in the public mind about Bush at a time when he had been riding high as a wartime leader.

And they had the cover of military experts leading the charge that the Pentagon was screwing up.

But few spoke out. Former Vermont Governor Howard Dean, who had staked his bid for the nomination on opposing the war, was the only vocal naysayer of the major Democratic presidential candidates. Clark, the most qualified of the Democratic candidates on military matters, was not as forceful as Dean.

But the TV generals were on the march. Their criticism of Rumsfeld and the White House war planners was at a fever pitch one day as I interviewed Senator Joe Lieberman on the campaign trail in New York's Lower East Side.

A self-described hawk in favor of the Iraq War, the Connecticut Democrat, of all his party's presidential hopefuls, was in the best position to question how it was being run. As a war supporter, Lieberman earned some credibility to raise doubts.

As Lieberman approached a gaggle of television cameras at a senior citizen center, I asked him about the rising criticism from military experts. Was the Bush administration naive about the strength of Iraqi opposition in the opening days of the war? What about Vice President Dick Cheney's prewar prediction that Iraqi soldiers would lay down their arms and run?

Lieberman took a pass.

"People were optimistic, but war is about unpredictable consequences," he gently noted. "The important thing to say is that we're there for a good reason. We're together, however long it takes."[13]

Moments earlier on other topics, Lieberman showed no such reticence. To a group of seniors angry about proposed budget cuts for their programs, he harshly attacked the Bush White House.

But like other major Democratic hopefuls, Lieberman ducked the chance to jab Bush on the war. Other campaigns turned down requests that day for an interview about the war's progress. "The boss is not addressing it," said one candidate's press secretary.

While politicians dodged and reporters on the ground in Iraq were muzzled, it was up to the military pundits to engage this debate. Retired U.S. Army General Barry McCaffrey, who commanded an infantry division in the first Persian Gulf war, even blasted Rumsfeld in the foreign press. In an interview aired by BBC, he echoed the complaints of other military analysts that Rumsfeld had ignored the pleas of Pentagon planners in his determination to launch a lightning-fast raid to Baghdad.

"I think he thought these were U.S. generals with their feet planted in World War II that didn't understand the new way of warfare," McCaffrey told BBC.[14]

The White House soon fought back. These military experts represented a gap in the message management of the war effort. Political foes had been easily shut down. Once the shooting started, any criticism of the war was deemed a slam on the troops.

News reporters had been subdued with the embedding system. They were getting unprecedented access to the troops but kept criticism to a minimum for fear of losing that access.

But the military pundits were another story. The White House had not thought of a way to control them before the war started. They didn't think it would be necessary.

Retired military types would be their friends, the White House calculated. How do you find anyone more pro-military than retired generals and colonels?

Indeed, antiwar politicians and many in the news media complained that the television networks hired so many ex-military officials. They too calculated that the TV generals would toe the Pentagon line.

Former *Washington Post* columnist Colman McCarthy, now director of the Center for Teaching Peace, railed against the TV generals in an op-ed piece for the *Post*: "The tube turned into a parade ground for military men—all well-groomed white males—saluting the ethic that war is rational, that bombing and shooting are the way to win peace, and that their uniformed pals in Iraq were there to free people, not slaughter them."[15]

Who knew that such men would turn out to be the news media's most vocal critics of the war?

But the military pundits were speaking for their constituency in the Pentagon, even if they were single-handedly driving the debate against the handling of the war. Many in the Pentagon were angry at Rumsfeld for overruling their plans for a larger force.

You can always count on bureaucrats to want more resources, and the TV generals were toeing that party line.

After a few days of hearing the military pundits complain on television, the White House pounced. Bush aides complained to television executives. Republicans in Congress spoke against them on the House and Senate floors.

Senator John Warner, the chairman of the Armed Services Committee, proposed a new standard of etiquette for retired military officers. His plan? Ex-military people should not be allowed to publicly criticize the military.

"I think they should follow the tradition of presidents, the commander in chiefs," Senator Warner said. "You do not see former presidents criticizing a sitting president during war."

The White House message was that the TV generals did not know the military's plans in Iraq. The implication was that if only these critics knew the real strategy, they would not have anything to complain about.

The Bush administration's counteroffensive peaked at a press conference with Rumsfeld and General Richard B. Myers, the chairman of the Joint Chiefs of Staff.

"I think for some retired military to opine as aggressively as some have done is not helpful," Myers said.

Soon, the military pundits were given new orders from their TV bosses. Erik Sorenson, the president of MSNBC at the time, explained it this way to the *New York Times*:

"We've instructed our generals to be careful not to speculate on what they don't know," he said. "And I don't know of anyone who has seen the war plan in our news organization."[16]

In short order, the White House muted the first round of criticism of its war strategy. A year later, the complaints of the TV generals became standard fare, as insurgents increasingly ambushed and killed U.S. soldiers. Even soldiers and officers serving in Iraq began to echo what the military pundits had said a year earlier.

Instead of heeding the warnings of these military experts at a time when something could have been done to fortify against the chaos that ultimately descended on the troops, the White House and its Pentagon chiefs blamed the messengers.

6

Who Will Tell the Truth?

Politicians who manage to be unanswerable to the media are in effect unanswerable to the public they serve. If this is a republic, defined as a system of leaders elected to represent the people, then shouldn't we expect those leaders to take questions about how they represent us?

I would go further. We should also expect them to tolerate criticism of their decisions without attacking the rights of those who criticize.

We should expect the news media to ask the critical questions.

Biased reporting happens, and it is a problem. But submissive reporting is the greater danger.

The public should be more worried about reporters who wimp out than about reporters who promote an agenda.

Helen Thomas was one of the few reporters in the White House press corps to ask critical questions before, during, and after the Iraq War. For that, she was effectively banned from view. She was ignored at the daily press briefings. She was no longer recognized for a question at presidential press conferences. Thomas had been a fixture in those press conferences since she began covering the White House in the Kennedy administration.

When Senate Armed Services Chairman John Warner asserted in March 2003 that military analysts on television had no right to criticize the handling of the Iraq War, he joined a successful White House effort to mute a critical debate about strategy at a time when serious problems could have been fixed.

A debate of the troop levels and resources in Iraq at such an early stage of the war might have led to changes that saved the lives of soldiers.

Even if such a debate would have changed nothing, any self-respecting democracy must encourage a free and independent news media to do its job before sending American soldiers to their deaths. It is the only way to be absolutely certain that there is no alternative to war.

Instead, most of the news media waited nearly a year to ask critical questions about the war. They waited until public opinion polls showed declining support for the war, when the daily toll of American deaths was at an all-time high. By then their tough questions rang hollow. It was too late.

If reporters don't do their job and let politicians bully them into submission, how does the truth get out?

We are talking about the truth here. It often needs a lot of help getting out. And in a democracy, the biblical saying is most apt: "The truth shall make you free."[1]

LOSING PUBLIC FAITH

Because very few Americans can come to Washington every time they want to get the truth from our politicians, we have the news media to do it for us.

Yet our society often dismisses the role of reporters as surrogates for the citizenry in dealing with politicians. Instead, too many Americans see reporters who ask critical questions of their favorite politician or political party as enemies of that cause.

Too many in the news media shy away from pressuring politicians. Television producers often worry that a news maker will not come on their shows again if they get too tough on them. Reporters sometimes worry that they will lose access to the halls of power if they speak truth to power.

As a result, the news media has lost the public's faith to serve as its surrogate. If the news media cannot regain the public's trust to speak for average Americans, we are in danger of losing our democracy.

The rise of Internet bulletin boards, called "blogs" in the Web world, creates the illusion that any American can fire up the desktop and hold politicians accountable. Not in our lifetime.

Blogs are a positive force. They rally public opinion, get people engaged, and sometimes drive stories that the news media missed or knowingly avoided. But they are not a substitute for reporters walking the beat at the White House or on Capitol Hill.

No blogger has the opportunity to rattle a president or a senator with a question he or she does not want to face.

DROPPING THE BALL

Even if the Iraq War turns out to be America's greatest moment, it left a sad legacy for the news media. The stunning failure to ask tough questions until hundreds of American soldiers died was one of the lowest moments in the history of our supposedly free press.

Perhaps the nation would have concluded that Bush was on the correct course even if the news media had been more critical before the war started. But at least the public would have known more about what the country was getting into.

A rigorous prewar drubbing from the news media would have put Bush in a stronger position once the occupation of Iraq proved to be longer and more difficult than anyone expected. The American people would not have been so surprised. Instead, Bush ultimately faced persistent questions and criticism and rising public doubt because his administration thwarted any informative debate of its actions in the early days of the war.

Before the Iraq War, the Bush administration asserted that the task would be quick and easy. Vice President Dick Cheney led the way on that claim, saying that the Iraqi soldiers would lay down their arms and run, that we would be greeted as liberators.

The rosy scenario faced no meaningful scrutiny before the war, even though there were plenty of doubters in the military world.

The nation might have found a less painful way to deal with Iraqi dictator Saddam Hussein had there been a more vigorous debate of Bush's determination to invade with or without international allies.

Only the news media could have provided that debate. But the questions either weren't asked, or if they were, as when Helen Thomas tried to do so, those asking the questions were frozen out.

The president's political foes backed off. They were subdued by White House threats to equate any criticism of the war with a failure to support the troops.

Antiwar advocates were not welcome in most newsrooms. When hundreds of thousands marched in the streets of major American cities before the war, many in the news media joined the prowar politicians in laughing them off as a bunch of kooks.

With news media subdued and dissenting voices stifled, the politicians had their way free of scrutiny. That is not democracy.

MEDIA GLORY DAYS

Today it is difficult to imagine an American president saying what Lyndon Johnson said of Walter Cronkite in 1968 when the CBS anchor reported on a trip to Vietnam and announced that the nation was losing the war.

"If I've lost Cronkite, I've lost middle America," Johnson told his press secretary, Bill Moyers, after watching the broadcast on February 27, 1968.[2]

No one in the news media has that kind of power anymore. To some, that is a good thing.

For starters, the big three networks had a monopoly on American eyeballs in 1968. More people watched their newscasts than at any time in history. In those days, everyone who watched news at dinnertime watched one of only three outlets—ABC, CBS, or NBC.

Today, the number of people watching the network newscasts has dropped by 60 percent since the day Cronkite spoke against the Vietnam War.

On February 27, 1968, Cronkite was not only at the zenith of his own career. Newscasts for all the networks were at an all-time high. And Cronkite was on the cusp of a decade of ratings dominance over his rivals.[3]

No one in the news media working today could sit down at the anchor desk or a computer terminal and reach as many Americans as Cronkite could on that day.

Cronkite had just returned from a trip to Vietnam, where U.S. forces had just been surprised and overwhelmed by the Tet Offensive. North Vietnamese forces invaded the soil of our ally, South Vietnam, and for a time even seized the U.S. Embassy in the capital of Saigon.

Antiwar sentiment in the United States was peaking. President Johnson was at the beginning of an election year.

Cronkite, who had earned his war-reporting credentials as a correspondent during World War II and Korea, aired a report on his just-completed trip to Vietnam and then concluded the broadcast with these words:

> Tonight, back in more familiar surroundings in New York, we'd like to sum up our findings in Vietnam, an analysis that must be speculative, personal, subjective. Who won and who lost in the great Tet offensive against the cities? I'm not sure. The Vietcong did not win by a knockout, but neither did we. The referees of history may make it a draw. Another standoff may be coming in the big

battles expected south of the Demilitarized Zone. Khesanh could well fall, with a terrible loss in American lives, prestige and morale, and this is a tragedy of our stubbornness there; but the bastion no longer is a key to the rest of the northern regions, and it is doubtful that the American forces can be defeated across the breadth of the DMZ with any substantial loss of ground. Another standoff.

On the political front, past performance gives no confidence that the Vietnamese government can cope with its problems, now compounded by the attack on the cities. It may not fall, it may hold on, but it probably won't show the dynamic qualities demanded of this young nation. Another standoff.

We have been too often disappointed by the optimism of the American leaders, both in Vietnam and Washington, to have faith any longer in the silver linings they find in the darkest clouds. They may be right, that Hanoi's winter-spring offensive has been forced by the Communist realization that they could not win the longer war of attrition, and that the Communists hope that any success in the offensive will improve their position for eventual negotiations. It would improve their position, and it would also require our realization, that we should have had all along, that any negotiations must be that—negotiations, not the dictation of peace terms. For it seems now more certain than ever that the bloody experience of Vietnam is to end in a stalemate. This summer's almost certain standoff will either end in real give-and-take negotiations or terrible escalation; and for every means we have to escalate, the enemy can match us, and that applies to invasion of the North, the use of nuclear weapons, or the mere commitment of one hundred, or two hundred, or three hundred thousand more American troops to the battle. And with each escalation, the world comes closer to the brink of cosmic disaster.

To say that we are closer to victory today is to believe, in the face of the evidence, the optimists who have been wrong in the past. To suggest we are on the edge of defeat is to yield to unreasonable pessimism. To say that we are mired in stalemate seems the only realistic, yet unsatisfactory, conclusion. On the off chance that military and political analysts are right, in the next few months we must test the enemy's intentions, in case this is indeed his last big gasp before negotiations. But it is increasingly clear to this reporter that the only rational way out then will be to negotiate, not as victors, but as an honorable people who lived up to their pledge to defend democracy, and did the best they could.

This is Walter Cronkite. Good night.[4]

It is difficult to imagine anyone of Cronkite's stature so plainly stating his opinion today.

This broadcast became the stuff of legend. Even today, those who criticize Cronkite as a liberal patsy cite this broadcast as prime evidence.

Yet in the context of the antiwar rhetoric at the time, Cronkite's comments were quite mild. He was drawing what he considered to be unavoidable conclusions.

DRAWING CONCLUSIONS

There is a small but significant difference between opinion and conclusions. I think we should allow journalists to draw conclusions when they have witnessed events that we had no opportunity to see for ourselves.

Opinion is a belief, according to *Webster's Dictionary*, a "belief stronger than impression and less strong than positive knowledge."

Conclusions are reasoned judgments, the "necessary consequence of two or more propositions taken as premises," according to *Webster's*.

We need more conclusionary journalism like Cronkite's in today's news media. Reporters should offer well-reasoned judgments. Opinion should be left to the believers.

Cronkite drew his conclusions based on personally visiting the war front and on his rich history as a war correspondent. He was one of the top American reporters in World War II, covering numerous battles in

North Africa and Europe for United Press International (UPI). After the war, he covered the Nuremburg trials and later served as the UPI reporter in Moscow for two years. He joined CBS News in 1950 to cover the Korean War as it began.

The February 27, 1968, broadcast stunned the nation. But most of all, it stunned President Johnson.

Just thirty-three days after telling his press secretary that he couldn't hold middle America without Cronkite, Johnson himself stunned the nation. He announced a halt to the bombing in North Vietnam and his willingness to talk to the enemy.

But the real kicker of Johnson's televised speech to the nation on March 31, 1968, was this announcement:

> With America's sons in the fields far away, with America's future under challenge right here at home, with our hopes and the world's hopes for peace in the balance every day, I do not believe that I should devote an hour or a day of my time to any personal partisan causes or to any duties other than the awesome duties of this office—the Presidency of your country.
>
> Accordingly, I shall not seek, and I will not accept, the nomination of my party for another term as your President.[5]

It is not too debatable a proposition to conclude that in one broadcast a network news anchor ended a war and a presidency.

Four years earlier, Johnson had unwittingly previewed what Cronkite concluded about Vietnam. In a taped conversation with his national security adviser, McGeorge Bundy, on May 27, 1964, Johnson voiced grave doubts about the growing war:

> I don't think it's worth fighting for, and I don't think that we can get out. It is just the biggest damn mess I ever saw. . . . It's damned easy to get in a war, but it's gonna be awfully hard to extricate yourself if you get in.[6]

Despite such doubts, Johnson escalated and widened the war with no holds barred. It took a journalist to bring him back to the doubts he had in the first place.

There is a line in Cronkite's legendary broadcast that nails both the purpose and the peril of journalists who cover politicians. "We have been too often disappointed by the optimism of the American leaders . . . to have faith any longer in the silver linings they find in the darkest clouds," Cronkite said.

A reporter's job is to shed light on the darkest clouds. Politicians can always be counted on to spin the silver linings. But sometimes the truth is not so pretty.

But if a nation ignores its hardest truths, we live in denial.

The peril in being the messenger of bad news is fairly obvious. Who wants to hear bad news? Anyone of sound mind prefers to see the silver linings. The bearer of bad news risks getting blamed for it.

Perhaps that is why the news media so willingly accepts a ban against pictures of coffins carrying the bodies of soldiers coming home from war.

THE "DOVER TEST"

In March 2003, on the eve of the Iraq War, the Pentagon sent the following "directive" to military bases around the world: "There will be no arrival ceremonies for, or media coverage of, deceased military personnel returning to or departing from Ramstein [Germany] airbase or Dover [Delaware] base, to include interim stops."[7]

The Defense Department order refers to the two primary military bases used for transporting the bodies of soldiers killed in the Iraq War.

With that order, the Pentagon eliminated a nagging public relations problem. Photographs and video footage of military coffins are vivid reminders of the reality of war.

Political and military leaders had long believed that extensive news media coverage of returning coffins during the Vietnam War played a powerful role in turning the public against the war. Since November 2000, at the end of the Clinton administration, the military maintained a policy of barring coverage of the returning dead, but it was mostly unenforced.

The Bush administration continued the lax enforcement during the Afghanistan War. Images of caskets from Afghanistan appeared on television and in newspapers until early 2003.

The March 2003 Pentagon directive marked the first time that the U.S. government strictly forbade such coverage. Witnesses say that planeloads of the war dead arrive nearly every day at Dover Air Force Base in Delaware. But the public does not see it, making it easy for anyone other than the family and friends of the deceased to pretend it isn't happening.

Concern about the public relations impact of military coffins is so high that in military circles they call it the "Dover test." It means that the need for war must be so clear to the public that they can withstand the sight of returning dead without wavering in their support for the war.

The official reason given for barring coverage of returning fatalities is that the government does not want to invade the privacy of the families. But a Dover military spokesman voiced the real reason in an April 2004 article for the *Boston Globe.*

"We don't let the media come on the base to perform the 'Dover test,'" Lieutenant Colonel Jon Anderson told the *Globe.* "That is Department of Defense policy."[8]

President Bush's team well remembered the public relations disaster that his father suffered while commander in chief during the Persian Gulf War. Television networks showed him giving a news briefing on the war in 1990 while a split screen displayed the scene of coffins arriving at Dover.

Although Dover mostly excluded coverage even before the 2003 directive, other bases did not. And even at Dover, there were many exceptions allowed through the years.

There was hardly a peep from the news media about this policy. The Pentagon directive was not even widely reported for months after it was issued.

A batch of photos of returning caskets did finally emerge. But getting the photos into the public domain required the efforts of an Internet-based activist and a woman who worked for a defense contractor. The activist had to file and win a lawsuit to publish the photos. The woman was fired for the publication of one picture.

The news media did not have much to say about the censorship of casket images until April 18, 2004, when the *Seattle Times* published Tami Silicio's photograph of twenty flag-draped coffins on a cargo plane. Silicio, a fifty-year-old Seattle native, worked for Defense Department contractor Maytag Aircraft at the Kuwait International Airport. She took the photo just before the planeload of U.S. war dead left Kuwait.[9]

Silicio, who had buried a son ravaged by cancer, felt a bond with the grieving soldiers who labored over the caskets. She later described the moment as almost like a funeral as the caskets were respectfully placed in the cargo hold of the plane. She had been carrying a digital camera on the job to record the momentous events around her for posterity.

The scene before her looked "more like a shrine than a plane," she later observed. She took two photos and the next morning e-mailed one to a close friend, who was deeply moved by it and sent it to the Seattle newspaper.[10]

The photo shows the coffins perfectly aligned on the plane as soldiers carefully tuck the corners of American flags around them.

When the *Seattle Times* responded with a request to publish the photo, Silicio thought it would be good to show the loved ones of the war dead how respectfully the remains are treated, even when loaded on a plane.

Maytag fired Silicio four days after the photograph was published, citing the U.S. military's "very specific concerns" about the violation of

Pentagon regulations. The company also fired her husband, a coworker she had recently married.

For a time, Silicio and her husband were a celebrated cause in the news media, appearing on nationally broadcast morning news shows and giving dozens of interviews. Within a few weeks, the phone stopped ringing, and they could not find work.

The *Seattle Times* photo editor had warned Silicio that she could lose her job after she sent it to her hometown newspaper. She didn't believe it, assuming that no one would retaliate for what she saw as a sign of respect for the war dead.

Months later, back in Seattle and still unable to find work, the woman had grown bitter.

"Before this, I had blind faith about my government," Silicio told the *Seattle Times*. "But I don't believe in this war. I believe in our troops, but I don't believe in the reasons for being there."[11]

Despite barring news coverage of coffins arriving at Dover, it turns out that the military takes its own photographs. Russ Kick, who obtained nearly 400 after filing a lawsuit against the government under the Freedom of Information Act, operates a website at www.thememoryhole.org.

At first, the government refused, but then a court reversed that stand. Kick placed the photographs on his website, and newspapers around the country published them.

Today, the news media is still barred from any live coverage of the returning dead at Dover. Photographs taken by the government can be distributed under the ruling won by Russ Kick, but that is not the same as allowing the media to cover the scene as a live news event.

The debate over the appropriateness of displaying these images is a worthy one. The best case for publication is that the government is clearly trying to manipulate public opinion by censoring unpleasant images.

Wherever you come down on the question of whether caskets should be seen, the truly disturbing lesson of this episode is how the news media played such a passive role.

Regular citizens took the lead in outing this censorship. One went to court, and the other got fired.

After the dust settled on Russ Kick's lawsuit and Tami Silicio's firing, the news media went back to playing by the government's rules. And the planeloads of unseen war dead kept landing, sometimes as many as thirty planes a day.

This time, the news media failed the "Dover test."

7

The End of an Era

It is the day the politicians won the war against the media.

"A few words now about the *CBS Evening News* and your reporter. After nearly a quarter of a century as the anchor of this broadcast, I've decided it's time to move on."[1]

With those words on November 23, 2004, Dan Rather announced the end of his reign as a network anchor. It also formally marked the day they drove old media down.

It seems likely that never again will a network news anchor be able to sway public opinion as Walter Cronkite did in 1968, turning middle America against the Vietnam War.

The seventy-three-year-old Rather's twenty-four years as CBS anchor is the longest tenure in the history of broadcast news.

Ten days before announcing his resignation, Rather began what he later described as an intense round of conversations with CBS management. He and his agent, Richard Liebner, went to the Times Square office of Les Moonves, the chairman of CBS and copresident of its parent company, Viacom.[2]

Rather told Moonves he was ready to quit. It was not an ideal moment for this passage, but events were spiraling out of control.

Two months before walking into Viacom headquarters to hand over his resignation to Moonves, the proud anchor had to go on the air and acknowledge fundamental flaws in a broadcast report that raised questions about President Bush's National Guard service.[3]

Rather and his producer, Mary Mapes, aired what they reported to be copies of four memorandums obtained from the personal files of Bush's Vietnam-era squadron commander. The commander, Lieutenant Colonel Jerry B. Killian, had since died. In the memos, he appeared to complain about pressure from higher-ranking officers to "sugarcoat" Bush's service record.

In the original broadcast of this report, Rather presented the supposed evidence as filling gaps in Bush's service record, including questions about why he had failed to take an annual pilot's physical.

The timing of Rather's broadcast could not have been more harmful to the president's 2004 bid to remain in office. Election day was just fifty-five days away.

Rather's description of the significance of the blockbuster memos on his broadcast was incendiary.

"They could help answer lingering questions about whether Lieutenant Bush followed orders and otherwise fully met his military commitments," Rather announced on the September 8, 2004, broadcast.[4]

Moments after Rather aired this report, the president's defenders on the Internet mobilized. They noticed that the documents shown on the air appeared to have been typed on a modern computer, not a typewriter typically used in the early 1970s.[5]

For nearly two weeks, Rather blamed Republican partisans for raising doubts that the memorandums were authentic. He repeatedly noted that the White House did not question their authenticity when they were shown the documents before the first airing.[6]

But on September 20, Rather backed down. He told viewers that a former Texas National Guard officer was the source of the memos and that the man had misled Rather and his producers about where he obtained them.

"The failure of CBS News . . . to properly, fully scrutinize the documents and their source, led to our airing the documents when we should not have done so," Rather told his viewers. "It was a mistake. CBS News deeply regrets it. Also, I want to say personally and directly, I'm sorry."[7]

CBS then announced a full investigation led by company outsiders. Rather's critics were not satisfied, observing that in his on-air apology he still did not fully admit that the documents were fakes.

A month after broadcasting his apology, Rather was with his agent at Viacom headquarters in Times Square telling the boss, Moonves, that he would step down as anchor of the *CBS Evening News.*

At one point, Rather's agent, Richard Leibner, excused himself so that his client could speak alone with Moonves.

"Dan was very emotional," Moonves later told the *New York Times.* "Clearly, this job and CBS News mean a lot to him. It was a very hard decision for him. Dan said to me, 'I'd like to do this on my own terms.' We totally supported him."[8]

Ten days later, he announced to viewers that in a few months he would no longer be anchor, although he would stay at CBS as a correspondent.

"It has been and remains an honor to be welcomed into your home each evening, and I thank you for the trust you've given me," Rather said.[9]

Rather's announcement came just two days after the forty-first anniversary of the event that first made him famous. In 1963, Rather was the CBS correspondent in Dallas on the day John F. Kennedy was killed. His steady reporting during the national crisis introduced him to millions of viewers and impressed network executives.

A Texas native, Rather started in journalism in 1950 as an Associated Press reporter. Within twelve years, he was the Dallas bureau chief for CBS. He later ran the network's bureaus in London and Saigon. He served as White House correspondent. In 1981, he took over the *CBS Evening News* anchor desk from Walter Cronkite.

RATHER MOMENTS

Beginning with his Watergate days as a White House correspondent challenging Richard Nixon at presidential press conferences, Rather was a favorite target for conservative critics.

The rise of the Internet offered plenty of opportunities for Rather's foes to share stories and impressions of his supposed liberal bias. Despite that reputation, Rather could be intensely patriotic.

Rather was actually presented as a shill for war in liberal documentarian Michael Moore's fiercely antiwar film *Fahrenheit 9/11*. It includes a clip of Rather hoping for a U.S. victory in a section intended to showcase mainstream media's prowar jingoism.

Rather seldom shied away from showing emotion, contributing to his reputation as a hot personality in the news business. As a guest on late-night comic David Letterman's first show after the 9/11 terrorist attacks, Rather choked up several times.

Just a month before the meltdown over his story on President Bush's National Guard service, Rather displayed his trademark candor in a panel discussion with other network anchors. He described the toll of conservative attacks on mainstream newsrooms like his.

"Fear has increased in every newsroom in America," Rather said at the Harvard University seminar in July 2003. He described the avalanche of e-mails and phone calls he gets on explosive stories.[10]

CHILLING EFFECT

Such pressure has a chilling effect on journalists. "You say to yourself, when you run this story, you're asking for trouble with a capital 'T,' so why run it?" Rather said.

In the same seminar, ABC's Peter Jennings and NBC's Tom Brokaw echoed Rather's concerns.

Conservatives "feel they have to go to war against the networks every day," said Brokaw, who retired from NBC's anchor desk in 2004.

Viewer statistics underscored the point. In a January 2004 Pew Research Center survey, only 24 percent of Republicans said they relied on ABC, CBS, or NBC as a main source of campaign news compared with 40 percent of Democrats.

Jennings connected the dots between the anger of conservatives and the powerful forces they could influence.

"I hear more about conservative concerns than I have in the past," the ABC anchor said. "This wave of resentment rushes at our advertisers, rushes at our corporate suites. I feel the presence of anger all the time."

Jennings had no way of knowing that the anger he described would topple his rival at CBS just a few months later.

Rather's "mistake in judgment" on the Bush story became a perfect distraction for Republicans worried that questions about the president's National Guard service were resurfacing in the middle of his reelection campaign.

VIETNAM REDUX

Many times in Bush's political career, the news media had tried to get the whole truth on the murky details of his Vietnam-era military service. The story kept coming back because the president and his team never fully answered the questions or definitively proved that he completed his service as he had said he did.

During the summer of the 2004 presidential campaign, Bush supporters reopened the door to Vietnam records by intensely questioning the validity of Democratic opponent John Kerry's military medals. The news media ran rampant with those stories all summer.

A group of Vietnam veterans who harbored ill will toward Kerry for opposing the war after his service bought television ads asserting that Kerry did not deserve his combat medals. Their claims were debatable at best, but they got a full airing in the news media and raised doubts in the minds of many voters, according to opinion polls.

By the end of this feverish run of Kerry stories, the Massachusetts senator could no longer use his combat experience as effectively as he had planned to do in the campaign.

Kerry supporters began clamoring for the news media to play fair and reopen the case on Bush's military service.

The *Boston Globe*, Kerry's hometown newspaper, and others in the news media began aggressively exploring the president's background. Conservatives complained this was a sign of pro-Kerry bias. While that may have been true in some cases, that claim overlooks how intensely the news media carried the charges against Kerry's service.

The thrust of the case on Bush's military service was that he used his privileged status as the son of a famous politician to avoid harm's way in Southeast Asia.

This was at odds with the Bush campaign's character sketch of their man as a tough guy who never dodges a fight.

There were two key points in question. Did Bush show up for duty as ordered while working on a political campaign in Alabama, and why did he miss a physical examination, resulting in the loss of his flight status as a jet fighter pilot?

No one ever proved that Bush was AWOL in the summer of 1972, as Democratic National Committee chairman Terry McAuliffe asserted during the campaign.

But neither could Bush aides prove that he showed up as he was supposed to do in Alabama. Witnesses contradicted each other. Some who served in the Alabama guard said they saw him. Others said he wasn't there.

The official records, once reported missing and then surprisingly found in the middle of the 2004 campaign, did not clear up matters. Pentagon records quietly released on the eve of the Democratic National Convention, when the news media wasn't paying close attention, showed that Bush was not paid for the period in question, indicating that he did not show up.

But the White House noted that the records also showed that Bush had accumulated sufficient service points in earlier months and so did not need to report for duty that summer.

This left the official Bush position on the questions in an odd posture: He showed up, but if he didn't show up, it doesn't matter because he didn't have to.

What appeared to be pure doublespeak invited another round of media scrutiny, especially after the news media had so extensively covered the nuances of questions about the validity of Kerry's Vietnam combat medals.

It was into this melee that Dan Rather thrust himself during the final weeks of the campaign.

The original broadcast of Rather's supposed evidence of undue pressure on Bush's commander went to the heart of the issue of Bush's failure to take a physical examination. The White House never had come up with an explanation for this. And now CBS was reporting that it had memorandums proving that the commander complained of pressure to "sugarcoat" Bush's failure to complete the exam and other obligations.

Combined with other recent revelations in the news media about gaps and questions in Bush's service, the story was on the cusp of expanding beyond the control of the president's campaign team.

Bush foes on the Internet and elsewhere had long spun tales about reasons why he missed the physical exam, even though it meant the loss of his flight status. The cadre of Bush haters claimed he was avoiding a drug test, suggesting that he was on drugs. Nothing of the sort had ever been proven despite years of such claims surrounding the issue.

Nevertheless, the Bush team knew this was explosive stuff.

What transpired is a classic example of the messenger blowing his own story and letting the politician in his crosshairs turn the tables against him.

When the memorandums in Rather's report appeared to be fake, the president's defenders had just what they needed to steer the story onto safer ground. They could make Dan Rather the issue.

Already the poster boy for biased reporting, according to those who believe the news media is out to get Republicans, Rather and his reliance on false evidence soon overwhelmed all the current stories about Bush's service record. Legitimate, well-researched stories by other news outlets instantly disappeared from the campaign news agenda.

Rather struggled to keep the basics of his report intact despite growing proof that the memos were fake.

"Those who have criticized aspects of our story have never criticized the heart of it, the major thrust of our report, that George Bush received preferential treatment to get into the National Guard and, once accepted, failed to satisfy the requirements of his service," Rather said in a September 15 broadcast of *60 Minutes*.

In that broadcast, Rather interviewed the woman who had served as the secretary for Bush's now-deceased commander, the purported author of the smoking-pistol memos. She both helped and hurt Rather's case.

Marion Carr Knox, now eighty-six years old, spent more than two decades as a secretary at Ellington Air Field in Houston. She was there in the early 1970s when Bush served, typing correspondence and memorandums for his commander, Colonel Jerry Killian, who died in 1984.

"I did not type those memos," Knox said, referring to the documents that Rather had reported on.

"You didn't type these memos?" Rather asked.

"No," she said. "And it's not the form that I would have used. And there are words in there that belong to the Army, not to the Air Guard. We never used those terms."

Rather goes on to report that the woman "believes the documents we obtained are not authentic."

But, as Rather notes, there is a "confusing twist."

The former secretary said that she did type a similar memo and confirmed that her boss was upset about preferential treatment for Bush.

"He was upset about it," Knox said. "And that was one of the reasons why he—well, he wrote the—a memo directing him to go take the physical."

Throughout the interview, Knox confirms the basic story that Bush got preferential treatment and that her boss was so bothered by it that he kept a "cover your back" file on Bush's failure to follow direct orders.

Knox said Bush's attitude was that "he really didn't have to go by the rules." She told Rather in the interview that other officers felt "sort of resentful" for his "above reproof" attitude.

"It was a big no-no to not follow orders," Knox said. "And I can't remember anyone refusing to—now, for instance, with the physical, every officer knew that at his birthday he was supposed to have that flying physical. Once in a while they might be late, but there would be a good excuse for it and they would let the commander know and try to set up a date for a makeup. But if they did not take that physical, they were off of flying status until they did."

If not for the all-consuming controversy about the authenticity of the base commander's purported memo, this would have been a devastating interview for the president's campaign.

But the secretary's extensive comments on Bush's failure to follow orders was completely lost in the following days.

Rather's story had not fallen apart. If he had solely based his original report on this woman's recollections and never mentioned the memos, there might have been a national debate about Bush and his service record instead of the one that mushroomed over Rather's reputation and credibility.

The messenger had become the issue, and his message was lost.

THE SON RISES

The president was in the clear. His National Guard service was off the front pages, replaced by calls for Dan Rather's resignation.

Bush won reelection without ever having to answer or even entertain questions about his military record. And he did so having watched his friends and supporters successfully undermine his opponent's military record.

It was a miraculous feat of political jujitsu. The candidate who had avoided combat during Vietnam benefits from attacks on the credibility of the combat veteran in the race.

This was made possible by the exploitation of a reporter's mistake. Even if Rather had not blundered in gathering the news, his reputation as a liberal would have been at the forefront of the Bush campaign's response. His mistakes made it that much easier to distract voters from the meat of the story he was reporting.

The demise of Dan Rather is about more than one anchor stepping down under fire.

It is a cautionary tale for any journalist to keep the facts in line and avoid giving the target of your investigation any reason to impeach your credibility and in turn undermine the point of your story.

It is the same as when a lawyer impeaches the credibility of the witness on a stand. If the witness can be shown to be incorrect about anything, the cross-examiner can create doubt about everything else the witness says.

The end of Rather's career as a network anchor also marked a victory for politicians who had spent years trying to dethrone the media elites.

Starting with the day in the 1988 campaign when Vice President George H. W. Bush attacked Rather, a crusade to turn the public against the media was under way.

Bush started the war. His son finished it.

8

Winners and Losers

Politicians and the news media are natural enemies. This is a good thing. With any luck, the public wins if both sides do their job.

The news media gets the truth out. The politicians face a level of scrutiny that either strengthens their case or winnows out the weak or corrupt.

There is an unstable balance of power between politicians and the media. The power shifts back and forth.

The pendulum of power now rests with the politicians.

Dan Rather's departure from the CBS anchor desk formally ended an era of media power concentrated in a few hands. The politicians had won the war against the media with or without Rather in the chair. But the longest-serving anchor in network history was their principal casualty.

No longer do three networks and two newspapers, the *New York Times* and *The Washington Post*, control what most Americans see and hear. In the old days, they set the agenda for the rest of the news media. Today, they struggle to keep up with a diverse media world that barely pays attention to them.

Dethroning media elites was good and bad. The media marketplace now includes more voices, points of view, and ideological beliefs than ever before. But without them, the media is divided and conquered.

With no one in charge of defining the media agenda, there is chaos. It is much like the breakup of the Soviet Union. The dictators are gone. Anarchy has replaced them.

Disorder diffuses power. Just as the Soviet states no longer have collective power to deal with the world around them, the American news media is a weakened force.

Divided and conquered, the old Soviet world no longer deals with the United States as an equal.

Likewise, politicians no longer fear the concentrated power of a few media giants. Today, the words of one network anchor could not possibly turn middle America against a powerful politician, as President Johnson said of Walter Cronkite in 1968.

But even the victors have reason to fear the chaos resulting from the dethronement of a powerful foe.

For instance, under the old Soviet regime, at least we knew where they kept the nuclear weapons. We knew how many they had and what they were targeting, and with satellite imagery we could detect any suspicious movement around them.

Today, however, much of the old Soviet arsenal is unaccounted for. Weapons slipped into the black market. They could easily be in the hands of terrorists. Are we really safer?

So it is with politicians and the diverse media world that emerged after the breakup of the old elites. Myriad cable news outlets, citizen websites, and bloggers now present an unpredictable threat to politicians hoping to control the flow of information about them.

Still, the politicians are better off. No one wants to bring the Soviet bloc back just because we might have been better off knowing exactly where their nuclear weapons were stashed. The Soviets also had the power to kill us all at once by launching those weapons.

OLD MEDIA VERSUS NEW MEDIA

Few politicians would want the old media power structure back in place. However, in some ways, it was an easier system to deal with. In those days, a president could call in a handful of journalists and shape conventional wisdom in an afternoon. Deals could be made.

President Clinton sorely experienced the new media's threat. Look at the contrast between the extensive coverage of his sex life and the conspiracy of media silence about President Kennedy's philandering.

In Kennedy's day, the working press corps at the White House was a very different breed than it is today. A small band of print reporters dominated the Kennedy press crops. Their ranks could easily fit into the Oval Office.[1]

Kennedy co-opted his press corps with charm and wit. Around the White House, some heard the buzz of stories about his many sexual affairs. A few even witnessed clear signs of his behavior. They ignored it because they didn't think it mattered in the performance of his job.

Clinton made the mistake of thinking he could play by Kennedy's rules. He was wrong. The White House press corps now numbered more than 2,500, more than double the size during Kennedy's time in office. Television news had long since supplanted print reporting as the prime source of news about the presidency for most Americans.

There was a vast media world outside the White House, much of it ideologically opposed to Clinton's political values. This new world had no interest in protecting a president from the exposure of his personal misdeeds.

But a "vast right-wing" conspiracy, as then–First Lady Hillary Rodham Clinton described those investigating her husband's sex life, was not the crux of Clinton's undoing.

Clinton's sexual adventures neatly met the needs of a modern media machine that is obsessed with entertainment. The breakup of media elites paved the way to this obsession.

In Kennedy's day, the media elites were guaranteed an audience. There was nothing else to watch or read. They intensely competed with each other, but as a group they did not have to struggle for attention. They could easily make collective judgments about what the public should or should not know.

There is no guaranteed audience for real news anymore. The explosion of cable television channels devoted to sports, music, celebrity gossip, cooking, movies, and sex created bedlam in the news marketplace.

To get attention, news reporting must be entertaining. Clinton's sex life was a fitting vessel for a perfect storm. It was the ultimate entertaining news story.

Still, Clinton won, and the media lost. TV ratings went up, for sure. More newspapers were sold. New websites became institutions, thanks to the Clinton sex scandal.

But after the dust settled, Clinton's defenders blamed the media.

"The Monica Lewinsky scandal exploded and suddenly the way to get to the top in the media was salacious gossip and sex scandals," former Vermont Governor Howard Dean, a Democrat, told an audience of Yale University students in November 2004. "There is no investigative journalism worthy of the name. Entertainment sells better than news."[2]

The crack hit of covering Clinton's adultery surely did change the image of legitimate news media. Parents had to worry about what their children read in the hometown newspaper. If they let them watch the evening news, parents had to be prepared to explain the meaning of oral sex.

The Clinton saga served to dummy down the news, and he benefited from it. Instead of focusing the story as a serious breach of trust when Clinton lied to the American people, the news media came across as obsessed with the sexual details. It appeared to be nothing more than a bottom-line competition for ratings and readers.

Although Clinton ultimately faced House impeachment and a Senate trial, the news media lost more. The public now saw them as no better than Hollywood gossipmongers.

It was the final severance of any connection between the mainstream public and mainstream media. The path was clear for George W. Bush to campaign for president in 2000 as the only hope for sending a champion of moral values to Washington. Bush successfully presented himself as best qualified to represent a Main Street culture that had been driven out of the nation's capital.

While this theme propelled Bush against Al Gore, Clinton's vice president, the news media suffered collateral damage. Bush expertly tapped into the view that the news media was hostile to the values of regular Americans.

A "HUGE ASSUMPTION"

More than a decade of comprehensive attacks on the liberal media, begun by Bush's father and brilliantly carried forward by Roger Ailes at the Fox News Channel, had taken its toll. The sex-obsessed mania of the Clinton coverage further established that the news media could not be trusted to speak for decent people.

The Bush team, once in the White House, operated on the correct assumption that the news media had lost its role as surrogate for the American people. They treat reporters as just another special interest group.

Media writer Ken Auletta relayed a telling story about Bush press relations in a January 2004 article for the *New Yorker* magazine.[3]

President Bush was hosting a barbecue for White House reporters at his ranch in Texas. Bush "let it be known that he's not much of a television-news watcher or a newspaper reader, apart from the sports section," Auletta reported.

"How do you then know what the public thinks?" a reporter asked. Bush replied, "You're making a huge assumption—that you represent what the public thinks."

Karl Rove, the president's top political adviser, further explained Bush's attitude toward reporters in an interview with Auletta.

"He has a cagey respect for them," Rove said. "He understands their job is to do a job. And that's not necessarily to report the news. It's to get a headline or get a story that will make people pay attention to their magazine, newspaper, or television more."

After examining how the Bush White House expertly manages the news, Auletta makes a profound point about the diminished role of the news media.

"For perhaps the first time the White House has come to see reporters as special pleaders—pleaders for more access and better headlines—as if the press were simply another interest group, and, moreover, an interest group that's not nearly as powerful as it once was," Auletta wrote.

AT THE MERCY OF SPIN

The result is a world where powerful politicians can spin away news stories they don't like. The public is more than ready to believe that the news media cannot be trusted, no matter how well supported a story might be.

Even the *New York Times*, once Mount Olympus in setting the news agenda, is now at the mercy of political spinners.[4]

In the final days of the 2004 presidential campaign, the *Times* reported a story that might have altered the course of an election when the newspaper was at the zenith of its power.

As the story broke, opinion polls suggested declining approval for the Bush administration's handling of Iraq. The war had been won but not the peace, as Bush's critics put it. Terrorists, called insurgents in the nomenclature of the day, were ambushing and killing U.S. troops every day. Many observers wondered how these rebels seemed to be so well armed with high explosives.

On October 25, 2004, just eight days before election day, the *Times* reported that over 300 tons of high-explosive materials appeared to be missing from an Iraqi weapons facility. Democratic presidential nominee John Kerry seized the story and ran with it. Here was evidence that Bush had bungled Iraq, Kerry argued. The failure to secure weapons was now endangering our troops.[5]

The Bush White House, aided by a cadre of conservative pundits, instantly challenged the accuracy of the story. The news media reported this instinctive spin as evidence that the facts of the *Times* story were "in dispute," which became the driving narrative of the story over the next few days.

Bold assertion plausibly maintained, as Aaron Burr once described a lawyer's job, is the primary rule for effective political spin. In this case, the administration asserted that the *Times* was wrong and offered but a few slivers of proof for their claim. It worked.

The Pentagon released satellite photos showing vehicles at the site while Saddam Hussein was still in power. This highly circumstantial "evidence" was meant to prove that he had removed the explosives before U.S. troops ever got there. Yet there was no proof offered about what was in those vehicles.

Still, this was proof positive that the liberal *New York Times* was just trying to sabotage the president's reelection, Bush's pundit allies argued.

Three days after the newspaper's story ran, ABC News produced footage showing American troops examining barrels of high explosives and leaving them behind unguarded. The videotape was shot nine days after Baghdad fell.[6]

Despite ABC's video confirmation of the *Times* story, the rest of the news media carefully presented the Bush team's spin as contradictory evidence of equal value.

The headline over a *Los Angeles Times* story read as follows: "Reporters Taped Troops Apparently Finding Munitions. A Pentagon Photo Implies Otherwise."[7]

The *Washington Post* overlooked the ABC footage and in its next-day story pursued the Bush angle that Kerry was inappropriately making an issue of the fate of the explosives. "This week's assertions by Sen. John F. Kerry's campaign about the few hundred tons said to have vanished from Iraq's Qaqaa facility have struck some defense experts as exaggerated," the *Post* reported.[8]

Fox News Channel's Brit Hume toed the Pentagon line, making no mention of the ABC video in his broadcast, telling viewers that "officials cite further evidence the material had been moved before U.S. troops arrived." Presumably he was referring to the satellite photos of trucks. He didn't say what he was referring to.[9]

Within a few days, the *Times* story became a hit on Kerry, thanks to the Bush team's spinning. Kerry and his friends in the liberal media made it all up, as the president's friends put it.

The bulk of the news media echoed that story line. By October 29, four days after the original story ran, the *Los Angeles Times* summed up the prevailing view in an article headlined "Munitions Issue Cuts Both Ways." Quotes from Bush and two of his political advisers were the only evidence cited to support the notion that Kerry was the one most harmed by the story.[10]

ABC's videotaped evidence confirming the *New York Times* story meant nothing in the contest against official government spin.

The fate of Iraqi explosives at that one site is not the issue here. What mattered in this episode was how easily the government batted the story away—and how willingly the news media equated spin with fact.

It is always provocative, of course, for a news outlet to run a negative story about a candidate in the waning days of a campaign. Many in the news media were going out of their way to balance their coverage, giving much benefit of the doubt to government spokespeople.

But to let the story twist out of focus as it did was going too far.

FEAR IN THE NEWSROOM

Fear too often motivates the media to back off a story. There is fear of reprisals from a powerful politician. Access to the politician could be cut off. Sources stop talking to you. Competitors get the best scoops. Balancing those dangers against the need to get the truth out is always a difficult maneuver for reporters on a high-octane beat.

Fear of the public also overcomes too many choices made by the news media. A time of war puts this fear in full relief. When bad news from the battlefield gets reported, many Americans see the media as unpatriotic. News executives worry about the effect on ratings and readership and thus the bottom line.

Keeping readers and viewers is a good thing for any journalist. What's the point if no one is paying attention? But when good journalism threatens public support, today's media executives often try to tame their newsrooms.

The need to make more and more money is causing a crisis in today's journalism. It is a trend that began years ago but seems to be getting worse. More and more media outlets have been folded into massive corporations, becoming internal profit centers that must post rigorously applied targets for increased revenue. If they don't, their resources dry up, and layoffs follow.

A rising number of journalists in America say their bosses are too focused on profits, endangering the editorial quality and independence of their work.

One pollster found a dramatic increase in the percentage of national journalists saying that bottom-line pressures hurt the quality of their news coverage. In the decade between 1995 and 2004, the percentage of journalists linking profit pressures to bad journalism rose from 41 to 66 percent, according to a Pew Research Center study.[11]

The pollsters found similar concern among journalists at the local level.

To see the effects of bottom-line thinking on your hometown newspaper, take a look in its archives. See if you can find any negative stories about well-established car dealers, grocery store chains, or department stores.

Auto dealers, grocery chains, and department stores are the prime advertisers for any newspaper. Few editors bite the hand that feeds their publisher.

I knew a columnist who once wrote an entertaining piece on pricing at a well-known chain of grocery stores. He found many inconsistencies among the stores, depending on the wealth of the neighborhood. Readers loved it.

Executives at the grocery company hated it. They complained to the publisher, who forced the columnist to retract the item and go to the company's headquarters to apologize.

Imagine the fertile ground that car dealers offer an investigative journalist. Can anyone seriously doubt that consumers sometimes get a raw deal when buying a car? But check how often your newspaper came close to exposing fraud or other misdeeds at a dealership that heavily advertises.

The news media lost the war against politicians partly because the need for bottom-line profits drives too many decisions made in today's newsrooms. A hot story can present a conflicting tension between the need to draw an audience and the fear that it might repel them. Advertisers are more aggressive than ever when it comes to putting pressure on editors and producers.

News consumers need to understand what's going on. Yet few of the journalists worried about these trends talk to the public about it. How could they? None would go on the air or use their publisher's pages to tell the public which stories they killed because executives feared the effect on profits.

Instead, journalists talk to each other about these problems but seldom in public. At most, we go to university panels and share a few inside stories. Sometimes those panels are carried on C-SPAN, and a few in the public get a clue.

Restoring public faith in truthful journalism would go a long way toward encouraging news consumers to stand up for crusading reporters when the boss is on their case.

People should think twice, for instance, before seeing a tough story on the Iraq War as a sign that the reporter is un-American. Yet polling shows that as the war progressed and the news media reported on its failings, the public increasingly saw the media as unpatriotic.

Public willingness to blame the messenger aids politicians in their never-ending quest to keep their own version of the truth in charge. And propaganda becomes conventional wisdom.

THE POLITICIANS WIN

When the news media loses in the struggle to find the real truth, only the politicians win. When propaganda rules the day, the American public loses the most of all.

The American public today is what author Noam Chomsky called "a bewildered herd." In his book *Media Control: The Spectacular Achievements of Propaganda*, Chomsky argues that a vast machinery of public relations experts, corporate chiefs, and media moguls are manipulating public opinion with greater success than ever before.[12]

Chomsky neatly sums up the view of self-serving elitists in the media and corporate world as follows: "We'll drive the stupid masses toward a world that they're too dumb to understand for themselves."

It is not that those in charge of our society get together and collectively organize their efforts to dupe the public. It is simply a case of their collective self-interest putting them on the same path—toward starting wars, cutting taxes for the wealthy, or downplaying a story about corporate crime.

It is time for the bewildered herd to get a clue. The American public needs to take a hard look at the role of journalism in their lives. Allowing the powerful to mute independent voices in the news media gives rise to propaganda.

Yet it is difficult for people to understand the pressures and promise of truthful journalism because the news media does a terrible job of explaining itself and almost never defends itself against attackers.

The first step toward better public understanding of a journalist's job is to come clean on our bias, our mistakes, and our fears.

9

Media Culpa

Has the mass media lost the masses?

Yes it has. Americans are more likely to believe a street salesman than what they see in the news media, if you believe the pollsters.

But one day (and for a brief time afterward), the public believed and trusted the news because the news media earned it in a time of national crisis.

Although September 11, 2001, was the nation's most tragic day in history, it was a bright moment for the news media.

The shock of terrorists turning planes into bombs on 9/11 created a panic for information. The news media delivered.

No cost was spared in newsrooms. Broadcast executives skipped millions in advertising revenue for wall-to-wall coverage. Ideology and partisanship disappeared. Republicans and Democrats were singing "God Bless America" together on the U.S. Capitol steps.

Free of ideological pull and bottom-line pressures, the news media delivered the facts in droves. There was no need for pundits. Opinions were irrelevant at a time when everyone just wanted to know what the hell was happening.

There are few times in history when all of the news media has everyone's attention on the same topic. 9/11 was such a time. And the public liked what it saw. Pollsters reported an unprecedented spike upward in the percentage of Americans who trusted the media.

In the days after 9/11, the percentage of Americans rating media performance as "excellent" or "good" reached a lofty 89 percent, according to the Pew Research Center, which routinely monitors public attitudes toward the media. Those who said the media "gets the facts straight" rose from 35 to 46 percent. These were the best grades for the media in a decade.

The media's post-9/11 favorable glow did not last. Things went back to normal by the summer of 2002, eight months after 9/11. The public's addiction to the daily news feed subsided. Business scandals and a plunge in the stock market now dominated the news. The cable talk show guests were yelling at each other again. Republicans and Democrats were wrestling over the coming congressional elections a few months away. And a debate over the Bush administration's plans to invade Iraq was just beginning.

By July 2002, the percentage of those telling Pew pollsters that the media gets the facts straight had dropped 11 percentage points, back to 35 percent, where it had been just before 9/11.[1]

Trust in the media is at rock bottom again. Indeed, it's at the lowest level in more than thirty years, according to Gallup pollsters. Just after the 2004 presidential campaign, Gallup asked the question they've been regularly posing to Americans almost once a year since 1972:

> In general, how much trust and confidence do you have in the mass media—such as newspapers, TV and radio—when it comes to reporting the news fully, accurately, and fairly—a great deal, a fair amount, not very much, or none at all?

A majority—55 percent—said not very much or none at all. Three decades earlier, in May 1972, that number stood at 30 percent, and the majority—68 percent—said they had a great deal or a fair amount of trust in the media.[2]

Put all the polls together over the past three decades, and you get a miserable picture of the startling decline in public faith. A variety of surveys since 1972 show positive attitudes toward the media falling from 68 to 44 percent in 2004. Negative attitudes rose from 30 to 55 percent (see figure 9.1).

How can the mass media properly function when the masses show so little trust and confidence?

It cannot.

STRUGGLING TO MATTER

Nothing the media has tried so far to fix this problem has worked. In the late 1990s, the media industry began experimenting with so-called civic journalism. Newspapers and television outlets launched well-funded efforts to make the news more of a public service.

The new civic journalism emphasized public deliberation, civic problem solving, volunteerism, and changing public policy. Explanatory journalism was in. Conflict journalism was out. This resulted in fewer stories about opposing sides gridlocked on an emotional issue and more stories searching for common ground on issues deemed more relevant to the average person.

But well-meaning explanatory reports on the dangers of radon in your home still pale in comparison to an old-fashioned street fight at an abortion clinic. The hot-button stories did not go away.

Although hundreds of news outlets tried civic journalism in one way or another, it did not change the overall decline in public attitudes toward the media.

So far, the only significant improvement in the media's image came in the weeks after 9/11.

Civic journalism did not change public perceptions because it did not address the core of the problem. Media bias and mistakes are what drove down journalism, in the public's view.

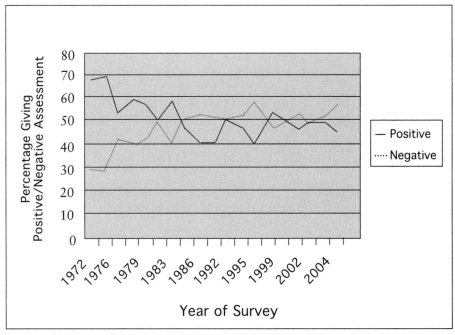

Figure 9.1   Public Confidence in the Press

A growing belief that the media is biased explains much of the over-all decline in public trust. It could even be the sole reason. Perceptions of bias grew more than any other negative factor regarding the media.

More than two-thirds of the public see the media as biased, no matter what poll you look at.

There is no escaping the fact that the public sees the media as too liberal.

A September 2004 Gallup survey found that 48 percent of those asked said the news media is too liberal. Only 15 percent said it was too conservative, and 33 percent said it was "just about right."

Not surprisingly, conservative Americans drive those numbers. While 48 percent of everyone surveyed see the media as too liberal, more than 60 percent of conservatives said so. This puts the media at odds with a large and growing bloc of Americans, considering that four in ten today identify themselves as conservative and that about the same number identify as moderates, while less than 20 percent identify as liberals.

I don't need poll numbers to see the growing resentment and anger at the news media. My own e-mail box delivers it on a daily basis.

MY HATE MAIL

As a news columnist and commentator in print and television, I often get the brunt of public unhappiness with the news media as a whole. The 2004 presidential campaign, a hotly fought contest between President George Bush and Democratic nominee John F. Kerry, kept my e-mail buzzing.

The anger is palpable, the attacks often personal and profane.

[The names have been changed to protect the writer's privacy.]

Frank A. writes, "Man, you are slow. The Dems didn't 'define' their man? Don't you realize that the more people learn about John Kerry, the less they like him? He now has a 36% favorable rating—not because he hasn't been 'defined'—but because he has—& NOBODY WANTS ANY PART OF HIM!!! Get a clue, will ya??"

Richard B. of New York writes, "Hey Redneck, I'll try to use small words so you will understand what I am saying. First, demoncraps HAVE said that President Bush has sent American soldiers to Iraq to die for Halliburton profits. Republicans have NEVER accused Kerry of shooting himself on purpose. It has been suggested by decorated veterans that at least one of his Purple Heart wounds was self-inflicted. Not intentional but SELF-INFLICTED. Imus may think your hokum is cute, but the liberal spin is getting old, quickly. Keep an eye on Dan Rather's career going down the shitter and see that it doesn't happen to you. You can fool even the possum eaters for just so long. Remember where you heard this first. LANDSLIDE!!!!

John D. writes, "You truly are an idiot. Your column equating the knowledge people have of Bush with what they know about Kerry is amazing. We know who Bush is you idiot and I suppose most of America knew of him before this campaign. You have the brain of a pea!"

Robert P. writes, "Have you ever done (written is too complimentary) any articles that are not hypocritical partisan political rubbish? I've not come across one. If you have one that you believe to be the case, please send it."

Richard K. of New York writes, "Was Craig Crawford drunk when he wrote the latest White House Trail Mix?. . . [Kerry] echoed the first JFK in rhetoric and ideas, and presented the Democratic view on values. Which, to the GOP's dismay, is much closer to the mainstream than their own right wing wacko take on the world. If you think that is too harsh, reread Mr. Crawford's article. It contains far more uninformed harshness than the previous sentence. Seeing the world as complex and without simple knee-jerk answers reflects reality, not confusion. The other side of that spectrum verges on ignorance and pig-headedness. I will certainly start to view his columns with skepticism now, and tell others to do so as well."

Occasionally viewers feel the need to get even. Paul B., threatening to spread Internet gossip, writes, "You refused to say calling the President a Deserter was wrong . . . so I am going to get you on the internet . . . you [expletive deleted] shill."

Some readers and listeners have either begun on their own or been trained by others to look carefully for biased reporting.

Ann T. asks, "How is [it that] you didn't mention the fact that while President Bush was comforting hurricane victims, your friend Kerry was getting a manicure?"

Jim H. of Arizona writes, "Mr. Crawford, in an effort to reveal the truth, I have contacted MSNBC and Congressional Quarterly about your status of an 'Unbiased' political observer and commentator. Your performances on Hardball and other MSNBC programs show otherwise. I do believe you are hiding behind your commentator status and truly carry favor for the Democratic point of view."

Jim continues, "You can come out and state for the public record that you support the Kerry campaign and let the public know your true intentions. Why be afraid of doing this, reveal the truth and let the public decide. Stand up and shout to the world that you are a liberal and another four years of George W. Bush would be bad for this country. Of course I know you would never do this, only because you would lose the big bucks and you would be thrown off the 'progressive television' gravy train. Surprise me, surprise the world, show some integrity and stop pretending to be 'Unbiased.'"

Larry B. of Florida writes, "You are smoking some sort of funny weed. Just wait and see how bad Kerry loses and will lose Florida as well. Go back to your liberal hole."

Robert L. of Florida, remarking on my opinions regarding the relationship between the forty-third president and his father: "Of course this dreck says much more about your own 'daddy complex' than it does the President's relationship with his father. When you get your medical credentials come back to this subject and try again. Oh, and try to wipe the smirk from your face. It's really annoying early in the morning."

Liberals join the fray too. They saw bias in favor of conservatives in my work. And just like their emotional counterparts on the Republican side, they are quite willing to hurl unfounded charges.

Kris L. writes, "You, like the GOP, are always trying to assign Mr. Bush qualities that he simply doesn't have. This smear campaign is NOT Bush's doing directly. The 'guts' are not his, but come from the evil empire of Rove and company. A fine distinction that you choose not to see. Let's forget Vietnam for a minute and look into other more compelling 'character' issues. Does this country deserve a bratty president from a privileged background who was a member of the pompom squad in college—who went on to further distinguish himself as a sucker-punching, rules-violating, rugby player—who further went on to distinguish himself as an alcoholic and coke-snorter—who has an arrest record—who embarrasses this nation continually when he is allowed to speak unscripted in public?—who admits that he doesn't read, an intellectual moron?—that the world despises and who lies to the American people to further his misguided, megalomaniacal, 'divinely inspired' agenda?"

Steve S. writes, "Lipstick on a pig is what that is. [Bush] is a pig for trashing the military and veterans and using proven lies to do so. Any thug can do that. It's not something to admire in a president. . . . You have to use your bizarre theory on thuggish behavior, where civil discourse is the mark of a leader, in order to find some way to shine a positive light on Bush's most crass elements and total failures."

Brandi B. of Florida, upset about my commentary on the political fall-out from hurricanes in her state, writes, "I will not question your intentions, but how dare you get on national television and talk out your ass."

Others seem put off by anything questioning the administration's handling of the war. Mark D. of Texas writes, "You want to jump on this administration for responding to terrorism . . . would you rather we just let the terrorist continue to train and plan another Sept. 11? More suicide bombings? More kidnapping and beheading of innocent citizens who are over in Iraq trying to improve the quality of life building schools, and hospitals? . . . I respect your right to freedom of speech . . . to print whatever you want to print . . . I hope you don't take it for granted. In Iraq, under Saddam's rule . . . you would not have had the same rights to make such statements against the government."

One hopes that those who e-mail such comments do not represent most people. But I fear the sentiment they express is far greater than most of us in the news media want to admit.

The crux of the problem in most of my own hate mail seems to be driven by the ideological or partisan bent of the person who writes it. When I criticize one side or the other, the believers on the side of the criticized see bias. Often they ignore what I said or wrote that was critical of the other side, even if it was in the same article or television commentary.

GETTING IT WRONG

Too many Americans seem to think the role of a free press is to agree with them. Our job is to get the truth, no matter who it offends. We don't always get it right because the truth is often hard to see.

I blew my prediction in a column on the 2004 presidential campaign. In the closing days, I thought Kerry had the momentum. "It's John Kerry's to lose," I wrote.[3]

Many readers saw this as proof that I favored Kerry. But I didn't vote for Kerry. I didn't vote for Bush.

I didn't vote.

WHY I DON'T VOTE

Many, if not most, Americans would disagree with my stand on this point. I have not voted since 1987, when I became a journalist covering politics.

I don't vote in an effort to stay neutral. I worry about the mental process of choosing sides at the ballot box. I fear it will make it more difficult to keep my observations down the middle.

This is a personal choice. I do not urge other journalists to shun voting to protect their objectivity. I am not even sure that my position is all that defensible.

But I came to journalism at age twenty-nine after a few years of dabbling in Democratic Party politics. I even ran for office myself in 1982, as the unsuccessful Democratic candidate against a Republican incumbent for a state legislative seat in Orlando, Florida.

I felt the need to go the extra mile in shedding my partisan background. That is why I chose to stop voting. And it became a habit.

In 2004, I did not like either candidate very much. I can't say for sure how I would have voted if I had done so. I like it that way.

As far as liberals and conservatives go, I see pluses and minuses on both sides. If I had to choose an ideology, which I don't, I might lean toward pure conservatism. But it really doesn't exist in today's politics.

A pure conservative, in my view, favors limited government across the board. This means less spending and almost unlimited respect for individual rights. On the hot-button social issues of today, a pure conservative would oppose abortion restrictions, favor gay rights, and probably even oppose the death penalty. Those are consistent positions with a genuine belief in controlled government.

The Libertarian Party is probably the nearest to pure conservatism in today's politics and would be my political home today if I chose one. But I don't choose.

It isn't a journalist's job to choose sides. This is the source of a major disconnection between the news media and the public.

Lawyers have the same problem when representing criminal defendants. The public cannot understand how or why a lawyer can represent someone if that lawyer thinks his client is guilty. But lawyers separate the question of guilt from the need to protect their rights so that those rights stay strong for the innocent.

Likewise, a professional journalist hammers politicians regardless of his or her own beliefs. It is more important to a journalist's job to critically question a politician's decisions than to worry about whether you agree with him or her.

EXPLAINING OURSELVES

It is time for journalists to get better at explaining their work to the public. Most Americans know that on some level a free press is a good thing but not enough see just how vital a role it plays in any functioning democracy.

Rebuilding trust in news reporting begins with coming clean on our failings and defending ourselves against unfair attacks. The public is used to a hubbub of self-serving voices in the media marketplace, but they seldom hear the media make its own case to the public.[4]

So many Americans think the news media just makes it all up. If only we were that creative. What's really wrong with the news media? It's not that we're biased. I know that is hard to believe. There are no secret societies—on the left or the right—where reporters design vast conspiracies and promote big lies to gullible readers and viewers.

The real problem with the news media is old-fashioned laziness— not physical laziness but mental laziness. Hardworking reporters will swim across a gator-infested river, climb up a greased pole, and dangle from the top by their shoelaces to get a front-page story. But ask those same reporters to sit down for an hour and think freely about what they're covering. Most would just laugh at such a preposterous idea.

10

How to Get the Real Story

As the dust settles on the war against the news media, what's left? Only two major types of media remain: advocacy media devoted to getting politicians of a certain party or persuasion elected to office and bottom-line media dedicated to attracting an audience big enough to make lots of money for its owners.

Independent journalism, free of political and economic pressure, is harder to find. If the news media is mostly dedicated to working for politicians or delivering profits to shareholders, who is looking out for what the average person needs to know?

"We don't have a vigilant, independent press whose interest is the American people," television broadcaster Bill Moyers said in 2004 on the eve of his retirement from PBS.[1]

There are precious few places for average Americans to go for the real story.

C-SPAN

C-SPAN is one of the few. Its unblinking eye offers a rare and uninterrupted gaze into the often boring reality of politics. Funded by cable television operators, C-SPAN is a reality show with a twist, devoted to substance and devoid of personality. Its founder, Brian Lamb, is an unassuming former disk jockey, Navy officer, and Senate staffer who set a rigorous standard for C-SPAN's unbiased coverage of public affairs without the usual news media distractions.

Occasionally—and almost by accident—C-SPAN gets the scoop.

I witnessed one of these moments while on air talking to C-SPAN host Steve Scully at the Republican National Convention in 2004. It was nearly midnight, and we were talking about that day's session, the first of four days for the GOP delegates at Madison Square Garden in New York City. The convention floor was almost empty of delegates. Scully was in the C-SPAN booth as I talked to him via the channel's remote camera on the floor. The lights on the convention podium behind me had been turned off.

While we talked, Scully suddenly interrupted me. It looked as though California Governor Arnold Schwarzenegger was at the podium, he said. It turned out that the governor was there to rehearse his speech to be delivered the next day. A quick-thinking C-SPAN camera operator aimed the lens at the giant teleprompter facing the podium from the rear of the convention hall.

And right there on live television, Scully and I were able to recite Schwarzenegger's speech for the C-SPAN audience nearly twenty-four hours before it was delivered.

That is not a life-altering scoop by any means. But it shows how C-SPAN's unobtrusive yet omnipresent cameras often catch telling moments that other broadcasters miss.

THE ASSOCIATED PRESS

Known simply as "AP" in the news business, the Associated Press is the most reliable starting place for the latest facts on a breaking story. Although AP works for the news media, which pays a fee for its wire service, there are many sites on the Internet to see AP stories for free.

Technically, AP is a nonprofit cooperative, which means it is owned by its 1,550 U.S. daily newspaper members. They do not look to AP as a profit center for their bottom line. Instead of profit, AP supplies content at a reasonable cost to its members. They elect a board of directors that directs the cooperative. More than a billion people every day read, hear, or see AP news stories.

The AP has a solid reputation for straight reporting. It imposes strict guidelines on its reporters, restricting their use of anonymous sources in stories and rigorously guarding against conflicts of interest. While other venerable news institutions, including many of AP's owner-members, face constant criticism for bias, AP seldom provokes such criticism. Its articles are devoted to getting as many facts as time and space allow. When an AP correspondent writes an analytical piece, it is clearly labeled.

National and local newspapers and radio and television outlets either co-own or pay for AP's wire service. Its work appears daily in more than 1,500 U.S. newspapers and 5,000 television and radio outlets.

Hundreds of AP stories a day roll across news media desktops. Much of the reporting you see on cable news networks and in newspapers comes from AP.

Because they pay for the service, many news organizations do not cite AP when relaying its reports. They feel they are paying for the right to pretend that AP's work is their own.

Take a look at your hometown newspaper's front page. Many of its national stories probably come from AP.

Although you might find AP cited at the top of a story, chances are that the citation comes at the end of the article on another page, if at all. Often, newspapers put only something like this at the end: "Wire services were used in this report." The newspaper might even cite AP or another service by name, but many times they just run the generic tag.

The disclosure means more than you might think. The reader has no way of knowing just how much of the article came from the wire story. It might just be one fact or a quote. But it could be that the wire source is the bulk of the article.

Radio and television news outlets are less likely than newspapers to offer any clues about the source of a story based on wire services. There are exceptions. On a hot breaking story, they will say, "Associated Press is reporting . . .," or they will see the AP report something and have their own correspondents check it out and then report the information as their own.

Because of the irregular way in which AP is cited as a source, it is difficult to precisely measure the wire service's full impact on the news we get, but it is likely that AP is the world's most influential generator of original news content.

Thanks to the Internet, news consumers can find much of AP's reporting for themselves. Websites such as news.myway.com have separate tabs for a feed of AP stories, and many newspaper sites provide AP headlines with links to the full stories.

The AP is as close as you get to "just the facts" in today's media. If they do get something wrong, they quickly correct it in an update moments after the mistake is discovered. The correction is noted at the top of the updated version.

There are other wire services. The British version, Reuters, is the next best source for straight reporting. The writing in a Reuters story tends to be spicier than the droll prose of an AP story. That is not always good. While more entertaining, the Reuters treatment of a story can come across as less factual than AP's more straightforward approach.

The French wire service, Agence France-Presse, is a good source for obscure details on foreign stories. Their bureaus reach further into the non-Western world than most traditional wire services. Many news watchers believe that AFP sometimes displays an anti-U.S. bent in its work. I've not found hard examples of that.

Like AP, reports from the other wire services are easy to find on the Internet.

The AP once had a strong competitor for reliable news, United Press International (UPI). But UPI struggled through a series of bankruptcies and a change in ownership starting in the 1980s, losing its market share and its reputation for unbiased journalism.

The Reverend Sun Myung Moon, a Korean evangelist, bought UPI from Saudi Arabian investors in 2000. Moon also owns a newspaper in Washington, D.C., the *Washington Times*, which bills itself as a conservative alternative to the *Washington Post*. Moon's properties, including UPI, have a reputation for leaning to the conservative side on most issues.

PUBLIC BROADCASTING

Economic and political pressure threatens the promise of public broadcasting. In theory, this should be "the people's home" for independent news free of commercial worries and ideological sway.

Supported by government subsidies and private donors, PBS on television and NPR on radio provide some of the most intelligent news and commentary on the airwaves. This economic model should free them of dependence on advertisers who rule commercial broadcasting.

But in reality, public broadcasters are often as commercially driven and politically motivated as their counterparts in the profit world.

A reputation for liberal bias cost public broadcasters much of their government funding. A long period of cutbacks began during the Reagan years as conservatives gained control over the federal budget.

Desperate for money and eager to shed their liberal image, PBS and NPR have dramatically changed the way they do business. Institutional charity foundations and large corporate donors rule. They are prominently featured on the air in a way that is not too different from advertising on the commercial side. Seemingly endless telethons are used to solicit funds from the public, but the take is a pittance compared to corporate and charity givers.

Editorial judgments are often secondary to the pressing financial needs of public broadcasters. Anyone hoping to produce a show on public airwaves must first have the money to pay for it. And if you have the money, they'll air it with few questions asked. Sometimes, shows on public broadcasting are barely distinguishable from infomercials, advertisements dressed up as news programs.

Public broadcasters try to put conservatives on the air in hopes of easing the attacks on their image as a home for liberals. But decades of catering to liberal viewers and listeners has made it difficult to find conservative personalities who can attract the public broadcasting audience.

Still, there are shows like PBS's *NewsHour* and *Washington Week in Review* that offer finely balanced news with plenty of time for in-depth reporting and discussion. NPR's morning and afternoon news shows deliver a compelling blend of news and features in a calm, no-nonsense style that can be a welcome change from the frenetic pace of commercial broadcasting.

But the wolf is at the door of public broadcasting. A shrinking economic base threatens its future, and years of confused programming have failed to expand its aging audience. In its current state, public broadcasting would not be much missed if it disappeared.

DON IMUS

Radio legend Don Imus is a surprisingly strong source for real news. On the air every weekday morning at 6 A.M., his quirky and often sardonic take on the news is as personal—and personality driven—as it gets.

I have a conflict of interest here. I do appear on Imus's show as a guest now and then. He doesn't pay me, so I feel secure in recommending him.

Imus is a strange breed of journalist, but I do consider him a leading professional in the news business. By constantly revealing his bias, his complaints, and sometimes his innermost feelings, Imus appears to be anything but an objective journalist. Sometimes, he can be delight-fully disrespectful about a public figure or an issue of the day.

But in the end you get a lot of real news on Imus's show. He loves the news. His curiosity about it is infectious. He grills a parade of re-porters, commentators, and leading news makers, persistently asking questions that everyone is thinking but is too polite to ask.

In the 2004 presidential election, Imus did something that every political journalist should consider. Early in the campaign, he revealed that he planned to vote for Democrat John Kerry. To most journalists, this is heresy. It proves bias.

But Imus managed to achieve a rough level of objectivity simply because he fessed up to his bias. Imus did not go easy on Kerry. If any-thing, he was tougher on the Democratic presidential nominee because of it. And occasionally Imus had a kind word for President Bush.

By leaning on the candidate he supported, Imus demonstrated what objectivity is all about. Being objective doesn't mean that you have no opinions. It means that you deliver both sides of the story in spite of your personal opinions.

Perhaps those of us in the news media could gain more credibility by making our opinions clear and then going forth and testing those opinions with critical reporting. That is a better approach than con-cealing bias, which is the conventional view of objectivity.

THE GRAY LADIES

Nationally distributed newspapers are a mixed bag when trying to find the real story. Known as "the gray ladies" for their dense type and tra-ditional feel, they face economic pressure in a more competitive world and are as beholden to their bottom line as they've ever been.

Many pursue a thinly veiled agenda. The *New York Times*, the original gray lady, has a reputation for a liberal point of view. So does the *Washington Post*. The *Wall Street Journal* offers solid and unbiased coverage on its news pages, but its editorial page is unabashedly conservative.

Beyond those big three, *USA Today* is about as careful as any in trying to avoid taking sides or crusading for a particular political agenda. Its editorial page is the most balanced in its league. The newspaper offers little of its own opinion on the editorial page, and when it does so, editors tap someone in the know, usually from outside the newspaper, to present the opposing side.

OMBUDSMEN AND CRITICS

Most newspapers now carry the writings of their own critics. Some are media critics in general, writing about the failings and foibles of the entire media industry. Others are known as ombudsmen, focusing on the shortcomings of the newspaper they work for.

Paying attention to these critics and in-house ombudsmen is an effective way for a news consumer to keep abreast of the latest media scandals or inside hand-wringing that constantly goes on. The news profession, despite its reputation for arrogance, is as thorough as any profession at beating itself up. You don't see lawyers or doctors devoting so much effort to airing their own dirty laundry.

The best source for daily monitoring of media insider debates is available online from the Poynter Institute at www.poynter.org. There you will find Jim Romenesko's column of current tidbits, commentary, and even a few secret memorandums making the rounds in the media industry.

THE NATIONAL NETWORKS

The news divisions at national television networks are still a solid source of real information. Shaken by attacks on their often parochial,

New York–centered view and an occasional left-leaning bias, the networks are seriously trying to clean up their act.

The financial resources available to network news chiefs, while dwindling, are still beyond anything available to most news organizations. With bureaus throughout the world, they can provide on-site reporting from nearly anywhere on the globe on a moment's notice.

When "the nets" mobilize on a big story, they have no rival.

Still, the bottom line rules national networks, sometimes undermining the quality of their journalism. ABC is owned by the Walt Disney Corporation. CBS is part of Viacom, a media conglomerate. NBC is owned by General Electric.

Shareholders of the giant companies that own the networks must be kept happy. Advertising keeps the revenue flowing at networks, and powerful advertisers are as aggressive as ever at showing displeasure about news coverage on the networks.

The morning shows are a growth industry in network news. Millions of viewers get their first news of the day from the *Today Show* on NBC, *Good Morning America* on ABC, and *The Early Show* on CBS.

I have been under contract with *The Early Show* as a political analyst since 1999. Despite the reputation of morning shows as primarily a venue for cooking tips, movie gossip, and exercise regimens, I found that the producers are serious about delivering solid journalism when they cover hard news. Generally, the first half hour of the morning shows, 7:00 to 7:30 A.M., provide a solid feed of real news that will keep you up to speed.

OPINION AS NEWS

Beyond the mainstream sources, news consumers who want the truth must deal with an ever-expanding world of openly biased news media. The best approach is to take in both sides and find the middle on your own.

Several media watchdog groups exist to help news consumers guard against bias, but none is truly independent. These groups approach their analysis as ideologues who believe the media is biased against their point of view. But their work is useful. With untiring research, these watchdogs provide a comprehensive review of the news media's many failings.

Opinionated journalism, although an oxymoron, dominates today's news media.

Rush Limbaugh led the way. His emergence as a conservative voice on radio ignited a massive following. He was a key factor in the Republican takeover of Congress in 1994. Limbaugh's daily diatribes against Democrats in the closing days of that midterm election proved to be a powerful force in pushing conservative voters to the polls to vote for Republican candidates.

Old media now pays close attention to Limbaugh. The man leading the next generation of network news anchors not only listens to him but has appeared on Limbaugh's daily radio show.

Brian Williams, who took over the *NBC Nightly News* from the retiring Tom Brokaw in late 2004, listens to Limbaugh from a radio in his office or tunes in from his car.

"I think it's my duty to listen to Rush," Williams told C-SPAN's Brian Lamb in a televised interview. "I think Rush has actually yet to get the credit he is due because his audience for so many years felt they were in the wilderness of this country. No one was talking to them. . . . Rush said to millions of Americans, you have a home. . . . So I hope he gets his due as a broadcaster."[2]

Faced with the success of Limbaugh and other conservative commentators, the Democratic Party and its liberal friends turned up the heat.

Although no liberal has built the following of a Limbaugh, ideological warfare now dominates the news media.

SHOUTING THE NEWS

National newspapers and television networks mostly avoided giving in to the cross-fire mentality in emerging media, such as talk radio and cable television. They paid dearly for it, losing market share to the upstarts.

CNN started it with *Crossfire*, a show that became popular in the 1980s for its carnival-like approach to public affairs. Hosts and guests on opposing sides of the ideological spectrum yell at each other with venomous one-liners. It is wildly entertaining, but that's about it.

The *Crossfire* style quickly took hold at other all-news channels. It is a genre whose time has passed, but most cable executives are still addicted to it.

ABC News President David Westin is a blunt critic of these yell fests, but he acknowledges that it works.

"There are very understandable reasons why," Westin told the AP in a 2004 interview. "It is easier and cheaper and, frankly, more vivid and attractive to an audience to put on very strongly expressed opinions."[3]

The host of a fake news show caused quite a stir in 2004 when he attacked his counterparts in the real world. Jon Stewart hosts *The Daily Show* on Comedy Central. Although based on actual news events, Stewart's show offers a hilarious barrage of jokes and sketches, thanks to an army of award-winning comedy writers.

In a profile of Stewart on CBS's *60 Minutes* in 2004, he unleashed an emotional and accurate attack on news talk shows.

"What has become rewarded in political discourse is the extremity of viewpoint," he said. "People like the conflict. Conflict, baby! It sells. *Crossfire*! *Hardball*! Shut up! You shut up!"

Cable news channels offer a contradictory mix of biased and straight news. It is fairly easy for consumers to tell the difference. The evening shows on cable news tend to feature hot personalities, sometimes with a clearly defined bias. They follow a rigid format of hosting combative guests on both sides of an issue and then letting those guests go at each other.

CABLE WATCH

During the day, cable news outlets tend to deliver straight news without the distraction of noisy show hosts.

At night, the all-news channels mostly go for the scream scene. On *The O'Reilly Factor*, Bill O'Reilly offers up a nightly dish of angst-ridden commentary on the Fox News Channel, with a populist tilt against liberal elites in Hollywood and Washington, D.C.

MSNBC's Chris Matthews is one of cable's hottest personalities, a bulldog interviewer whose over-the-top energy is routinely and lovingly satirized on NBC's *Saturday Night Live*. In the spirit of full disclosure, I do get paid to appear on Chris's show, *Hardball*. Despite that, I can honestly say that there is nothing more challenging than submitting to one of Chris's on-air exams. You never know what he'll ask, and your points had better be well supported. Chris can instantly find the holes in anyone's argument, and he never hesitates to point them out.

There are notable exceptions to the scream scene on prime-time cable news.

Greta Van Susteren, who became famous as a legal commentator during O. J. Simpson's murder trial, maintains order on her nightly show aired by the Fox News Channel. On CNN, network veteran Aaron Brown is a calming presence with an old media style, while Anderson Cooper aims for the younger set with a magazine-style show.

MSNBC's Keith Olbermann presents another conflict of interest for me. I often appear on his show and get paid for it. But even so, indulge my kudos for him. With a sharp wit and a dead-on alarm system for outing propaganda, Olbermann is funny and illuminating. In some ways, he runs the reality version of Jon Stewart's fake show on Comedy Central.

To get the whole story on cable talk shows, a partisan viewer should watch hosts they disagree with. It's good for you. Listening to the other side's arguments might strengthen your own point of view or alert you to important weaknesses in your beliefs.

If you are a die-hard liberal, watch Bill O'Reilly on the Fox News Channel or pay special attention to the channel's conservative commentator Sean Hannity, who cohosts a show with his liberal counterpart Alan Colmes.

If you are a prowar conservative, watch Chris Matthews on *Hardball*. Matthews was intensely critical of the Iraq War before it began. His background as a Democratic partisan occasionally shows, which is fine. Matthews is always quite clear about his own point of view.

On cable, the Fox News Channel is a reliable alternative to mainstream coverage. Its style comes from its owner, Rupert Murdoch, an Australian media tycoon who revolutionized British media before taking on the American market. Murdoch makes no secret of his conservative leanings, and his newspapers and television outlets reflect those leanings.

During the Iraq War, for instance, the Fox News Channel was the most careful to use language that was sure to please the White House when referring to our armed forces on the ground. Fox was alone among its competitors in using the label "multinational forces" when reporting on U.S. troops. This was quite generous to the Bush administration's desire to portray our troop presence as part of an international coalition.

Roundly criticized for favoring conservatives and Republicans, Fox News Channel's rise was predicated on the notion that the mainstream media was mostly liberal and that consumers deserved more. A mass of viewers obviously agreed. In just a few years, the Fox News Channel supplanted CNN as the leading cable news channel.

MSNBC, where I work as a contributor, is the only cable channel able to tap into the massive resources of a national network, NBC. On major stories, especially in other countries where NBC has bureaus, MSNBC often can get the most information and more quickly. Co-owned by the Microsoft Corporation, MSNBC began anew in 2004 under the management of network veteran Rick Kaplan.

CNN is the granddaddy of cable and a powerhouse for international coverage. Owned by Time-Warner, it is the original cable news shop but lost its dominant position to the Fox News Channel. CNN's *Headline News*, a separate channel devoted to a fast feed of straight reporting, is one of the most efficient ways to catch up on the day's news.

THE INTERNET

Surfing the Internet can be a horrible way to get the real story. Gossip rules the Web. Gossip is always enticing because it is news you can remember. It also can be nothing but lies. Often, it is very difficult to discern the difference between truth and lies on the Internet.

The vast supply of raw information on the Internet is nothing short of a revolution in giving consumers their own news feed. The gatekeepers of old media were almost put out of work.

Matt Drudge symbolizes the revolution in how Americans get their news. He is a genuine pioneer. Few saw the potential for the Internet as a primary news source until Drudge came along in the 1990s. On the controversial side, Drudge clearly favors conservative and Republican causes, but he does not hide it.

The secret of Drudge's phenomenal success is that he is a highly skilled news editor, although his fame stems from a willingness to push gossipy stories that might or might not turn out to be true. He became famous as the first to publish Monica Lewinsky's name in the early days of President Clinton's sex scandal. He is a pariah to professional journalists who see pure evil in his mischief, but many read his site anyway.

Drudge's strength as a news editor is overlooked, even though the vast readership of his Web page, drudgereport.com, proves the point.

Updated continuously throughout the day and night, the site nearly always features a riveting display of stories on topics ranging from Hollywood celebrities to political scandals.

Although Drudge writes his own snappy headlines, the stories on his Web page mostly come from legitimate news sources and include direct links to those sources. You don't have to accept Drudge's take on a story, which he tends to lace into the headline he writes for the story. You can simply click the link and read it for yourself.

When Drudge pursues his own stories or sources, it is clearly labeled. Those are the stories that earned his reputation for spreading unconfirmed gossip. But the strength of his work is in the reliability of his website for a quick and constantly updated read of interesting stories with links to the original sources.

Drudge's daily collection of linked news represents the best that the Internet can do for a news consumer. It is a delivery tool. It is not as good at generating its own content.

That is Drudge. His actual news feed is indispensable. It is his own reporting that gets him into trouble.

The Internet is a godsend for finding the best content that is produced by conventional news organizations. The unconventional stuff on the Web is loads of fun, but it is dicey when it comes to getting solid information.

News search engines on the Internet should be in every news consumer's toolbox, on the Favorites list of your Web browser.

The best I've found is news.google.com. It constantly and automatically combs the Internet for news, delivering blurbs and links to both conventional and unconventional news sources. You can set up permanent search words to direct the engine to look for certain types of stories, display them on your own Web page, and even automatically e-mail those stories directly to you.

There are plenty of news search engines available. Any one of them represents a miraculous step forward in allowing consumers to craft their own news feed.

For those with money, there are digesters available who do the surfing for you.

The Hotline, an online political digest where I worked for six years, is the best known of the subscriber-only sites. A dozen or more writers and editors begin surfing at dawn, by noon producing an exhaustive digest of hundreds of news sources.

Television networks now provide free news digests but naturally tend to emphasize their own reporting.

ABC's *The Note* keeps a daily pulse on conventional news wisdom. Its daily online list of links and blurbs on news coverage dwells mostly on the big feet of the news media. Its commentaries, at the beginning of each report, provide an accurate read on the current thinking of news media elites.

CBS takes a different tack, pitching *Washington Wrap* to a mass audience. Produced by the network's Washington-based political unit, it delivers a one-page series of blurbs on the day's hard news. Most days it is a near-perfect preview of what you'll be seeing on any network news show that evening.

NBC's *First Read* also has its own characteristics. Here you will get a peek into news gathering at a network. Like ABC's *The Note*, it is a much longer read than the CBS digest.

Reading NBC's entrant in this genre is like going to the network's morning news meeting. *First Read* previews what reporters at NBC and MSNBC are working on. There are lots of tidbits about where their stories are going and what is likely to lead their newscasts that night and the next morning. Like the other network news digests, NBC also cites links to newspaper articles and other sources for top stories of the day.

These online news digests are leading the way in showing network bosses how to use the Internet. You will find more detail in them than usually appears on the network's televised broadcasts.

OLD MEDIA'S COMEBACK TRAIL

Websites like those now in development at the networks could save their news divisions. After a long period of experimenting with delivering video on their sites, they stepped up those efforts in the 2004 presidential campaign.

The Internet is a long way from replacing cable and broadcast as the primary delivery tool for television news, but that could be where it is going. It would happen in a nanosecond if it ever made sense for advertisers to spend as much for Internet delivery as they pay now for cable and broadcast delivery. And there are signs that the mass market is headed for the Internet.

The technical feasibility for networks to deliver video to a mass audience is here. In 2004, the number of residential consumers with high-speed Internet at home topped 50 percent for the first time. This so-called broadband service allows efficient delivery of video that almost rivals the quality of conventional broadcast delivery.[4]

Will consumers watch television on the Internet? Not yet, but we do know that they are increasingly sacrificing their time watching television in favor of going online. A rising number of Americans are spending more time on their computers and less time watching television, according to a recent Stanford University study. Internet users spend more than three hours a day online while spending less than two hours watching television. For every hour spent online, consumers are reducing the amount of time they watch television by ten minutes, the study found.

If these statistics represent a trend, television executives must look to the Internet to capture the eyeballs they are losing. When advertisers get on board, they will waste no time in doing so.

Newspaper websites are also on the march. So far, most have resisted the bottom-line urge to seek a subscription price for reading the daily news on the Internet. But to search their archives, you will likely have to pay.

In most cities, it is not difficult to craft your own electronic newspaper using your hometown paper. You can set up a page that reflects your interests, and it's there every day with a fresh supply of customized news.

If television networks and major newspapers continue expanding their online presence, old media has a chance to come back. The failure of Internet-only news media to provide consistently reliable information paves the way for old media to revive traditional journalism online.

The *Washington Post* took an important step in this direction in 2004, buying *Slate*, an Internet newsmagazine once heralded as new media's battering ram against old media. Founded by the Microsoft Corporation in 1996, *Slate* was reaching an audience of 6 million online readers when the *Post* bought it eight years later.[5]

In one transaction, the *Post* roughly doubled the reach of its online properties to more than 10 million readers a month.

The *Post* deployed a tactic that other well-financed old media might duplicate: If you can't beat them, buy them.

As the Internet's market of consumers becomes more mainstream, the power of old media's corporate branding becomes a mighty asset. And the political pulse of the Internet audience could change, from its libertarian and conservative leanings to a more middle-of-the-road spot.

The Internet's first decades attracted early adapters to technology or wealthier people who could afford computers and Internet service at home.

Early adapters tend to be unconventional thinkers, drawn to the rebellious nature of Internet media sources trying to dethrone old media. Wealthier users tend to be Republican voters. This resulted in an Internet audience with a decidedly conservative bent on political issues.

Middle- and lower-income Americans originally had little access to the Internet. That is rapidly changing.

More liberal Americans and mainstream consumers accustomed to brand-name news are getting on the Internet. One day, the old media could muscle its competitors off the Internet by completely dominating the medium.

Old media can conquer the Internet with straight and reliable reporting if its new bosses, reporters, and on-air talent learn the hard lessons of their predecessors. Any hint of arrogance or a left-leaning agenda will doom old media's chances on the Internet. And the politicians will pounce again.

If old media's real journalists go online and earn back the public's trust, they could get back to where they belong, holding politicians accountable. Consumers would win, and freedom of the press could make a comeback.

11

What Now?

Professional journalism is not dead. Traditional news media will survive.

But for the sake of truth in our politics, it is time for the news media, politicians, and the public to rethink their social contract. Each bears a measure of responsibility for what's gone wrong, and each plays a role in making it better.

Politicians must honor the role of a free press in democracy in their deeds and not just in their rhetoric. The public must try to learn the difference between a legitimate criticism of media behavior and a politically motivated attack designed to clear the path for propaganda.

None of this can happen unless the news media takes the lead to restore public faith in professional journalism. Thankfully, the U.S. Constitution prevents the complete destruction of a free press. This allows the news media a chance to overcome its failings and get back to a place where the public respects—and protects—its role.

Decades of attacks by politicians and the miserable failures of shoddy journalists cannot destroy an institution that enjoys more legal protections than any other in American society. If the nation's founders had not included the First Amendment in the Constitution, the news media might disappear as a free and independent source of truth.

But legal protections are meaningless when the public has so little faith in what journalists report.

The news media's privileged legal status comes with a price. It is up to the press to guard its freedom by earning the public's trust. If no one can legally force journalists to do their job ethically and honestly, they must be ever vigilant about policing themselves in a manner that the public understands and appreciates.[1]

That is happening. There is an upside to the public flogging of the news media in recent years.

TAKING THE LEAD

Humiliation begets humility. The demise of the news media's arrogant and secretive old guard is forcing a transparency of the process of news gathering that is healthy and beyond anything in the history of American journalism.

Whenever a prominent journalist or news outlet stumbles, there is no hiding it.

"Just a few years ago, many of these issues would have been fodder for low-circulation academic and trade journalism magazines," *USA Today* media critic Peter Johnson wrote in 2004. "Now, those topics get headlines and airtime in major news outlets, driven by partisans who keep a particularly close watch."[2]

The fraudulent or incompetent are rooted out with lightning speed, and it is often done far more ruthlessly than what wrongdoing politicians experience. When an elected official goes bad, it usually takes a year of congressional hearings, independent investigations, and perhaps a court action or a return to the ballot box to finally exorcise them from public life.

Justice is much swifter for journalists. When it happens, the profession gets stronger. When weakness cannot be hidden, the weak become stronger by fixing what's wrong.

This new age of media self-policing led to the swift firing of a *USA Today* reporter whose fraudulent work had been overlooked for years. In 2004, a panel of independent editors found longtime *USA Today* correspondent Jack Kelley guilty of "years of fraudulent news reporting." Even more damning, the panel concluded that "newsroom managers at every level" had ignored "numerous, well-grounded warnings that he was fabricating stories, exaggerating facts and plagiarizing other publications."

Kelley resigned before the report was under way, and afterward two top *USA Today* editors were ousted.

The Kelley incident displays the full continuum of the change in media behavior, from once hiding flaws to now exposing them and rooting them out. We know that in the old days Kelley's failings were tolerated. That is what the panel concluded. But in today's more sensitive environment, he was fired along with those who had protected him.

USA Today and CBS ushered in a welcome trend by appointing independent panels to investigate wrongdoing. Journalists are always clamoring for independent investigations of politicians but seldom even considered it for themselves. Only by seeking transparent and truly independent inquiries of allegations can the news media inspire trust that the rest of their reporting is valid.

A telling and hopeful signpost for the road back to news media legitimacy could be seen in the extensive coverage of the early 2005 release of the independent report on CBS's use of an unsubstantiated memo to question President Bush's National Guard service. The independent panel's report was anticipated and covered as widely as an investigation of a president might be.

Independent and well-publicized investigations should become routine whenever serious and well-founded charges are made against a journalist.

As with politicians, the threat of immediate exposure is more effective than rules and regulations in preventing bad behavior. Rules are made to be broken, but knowing that plagiarism or conflicts of interest will no longer be swept under the rug will give pause to any journalist tempted toward the dark side.

ACKNOWLEDGING BIAS

Political bias is a tough case. The rule for conventional reporters is never to reveal your bias, if you have one. If you are covering a campaign and favor a particular candidate, you are not supposed to say so. Instead, the professional journalist with a bias is supposed to take special care to objectively report the story. If your bias is not evident in the story, then the public is well served and there is no problem, under the old rules.

The old rules aren't working. The public is as attuned as ever to even the slightest signs of bias, real or imagined.

I think journalists should publicly reveal any bias that is pertinent to their reporting. In today's world, it is not enough to produce a perfectly objective report and expect the public to believe you have not slanted it in some way.

Revealing a bias does not mean a journalist cannot be honest and forthright about the shortcomings of people and ideas they favor. Indeed, that honesty will be more appreciated and noticed if the audience knows your bias.

Earlier in this book, I wrote about my somewhat controversial efforts to avoid bias in my political commentary: I don't vote.

I get many arguments from journalists and the public about this choice, and I can appreciate how it makes me seem unpatriotic or apathetic or downright un-American. So I don't necessarily recommend this choice to others. But I do find it helpful in covering a campaign to take myself out of the fray by never even going through the mental process of picking a candidate in the balloting booth.

I am exploring ways to reveal my bias when it's important to what I am writing or commenting about. It isn't easy. I am trying to preface a remark or a written passage with a quick take on where I am coming from. It is a work in progress, but I am convinced that journalists no longer have the luxury of pretending that we have no opinions.

Our opinions, when disclosed, should be presented as context for our commentary or reporting. Merely revealing our point of view is different than advocating our beliefs. When we become advocates, we are politicians, not journalists.

But hiding our point of view creates suspicion that we are secretly advocating a cause. Fessing up to our beliefs would remove the suspicion, especially if news consumers see us get tough on politicians and ideas we've publicly said we support.

Editors and reporters at the online *Slate* magazine did this at the end of the 2000 and 2004 presidential campaigns, disclosing how they would vote. Each wrote an explanation of their choice.

Slate editor Jacob Weisberg explained the move to readers as a desire to show "the distinction between opinion and bias." Rather than bury their views, Weisberg wrote, "we cultivate and exhibit them." He spoke for a growing number of journalists in asserting that "we can openly express what we think and still be fair."[3]

If we are as objective about what we support as we are about what we don't support, the public is more likely to believe in our reporting. It is an odd twist of mind to reveal bias in order to remove bias, but these are odd times for the news media.

POLITICIANS ON THE LOOSE

Many of today's politicians are out of control. They won the war against the news media, but they want more.

We learned in early 2005 that the U.S. Department of Education paid a pundit, Armstrong Williams, to advocate certain legislation.

Some federal agencies create their own television news services, hiring professional-looking anchors to deliver stories and feed them to news outlets. Incredibly, local news affiliates often run these video press releases without explanation. To the public, these reports look like legitimate news instead of what they really are: pure propaganda.

Of course, it is outrageous for any news organization to air such reports. But local television stations, facing economic pressures, are often too willing to accept free programming of this sort.

Just because the government can get away with such shenanigans is no reason for it be done. Politicians share a responsibility to ensure that the public is not duped, even if a shoddy news outlet is willing to distribute propaganda.

Politicians must really honor the freedom of the press and the right of the public to get the truth. They will always say so with words but seldom do so in deeds.

Instead, politicians often act as though the free press is an enemy of democracy instead of its very guardian. It will always be thus. Many politicians are famously egocentric, unwilling to bear any criticism. The difference these days is that politicians have persuaded the public to see the media as the enemy.

The political challenge facing Americans is to begin seeing this dispute in a very different way. The politician who seeks to undermine the role of the free press is the true enemy of democracy.

Only the public can change this behavior pattern. In a healthy democracy, politicians get away only with what voters allow.

When a politician dodges questions by attacking or banning the questioner, the public should at least pause a moment before getting sucked into the politician's sly effort to blame the messenger.

LET US BE RUDE AGAIN

At the turn of the twentieth century, Chicago satirist Finley Peter Dunne recoined a biblical phrase that reporters since have famously paraphrased and repeated as their call to arms: "The job of the newspaper is to comfort the afflicted and afflict the comfortable." Dunne originally wrote the line in the Irish dialect of his alter ego, "Mr. Dooley," a fictional bartender with a keen eye for politics and the human condition.[4]

Dunne actually meant the observation to be critical of the news media's vast power in his day. His point was that it was supremely arrogant for journalists to think they could be so noble as to afflict the comfortable and comfort the afflicted.

But over the decades, the quote has become a mantra for brave journalism. I prefer this revised meaning, with apologies to "Mr. Dooley."

The powerful can take care of themselves, which is why journalists should give them a hard time. And the public should give us the space to do this job.

There was a time when the average person would watch a politician duck a question and immediately say, "He didn't answer the question." Today, people are more likely to say, "That's a rude question."

The public must let journalists ask rude questions again. Indeed, we should celebrate it, even when we totally disagree with the thrust of the question. It is good and healthy and, yes, even entertaining to watch a powerful politician get a fierce grilling. It's democracy at its best.

I often wish we could import the British tradition of "question time" for the prime minister in Parliament. Thanks to frequent airings on C-SPAN, Americans get to see what happens when a head of state faces tough questions without staff or teleprompters.

Of course, in Parliament it is the politicians of a prime minister's opposing party posing the rude questions. But the British public gets a chance to see a dramatic showcase of their leader's strengths and weaknesses. Prime Ministers Margaret Thatcher and Tony Blair displayed such skill and humor in these sessions that it actually made them more popular.

"Question time" is a healthy exercise for British democracy, but sadly there is no counterpart in American democracy. There should be.

Presidents get questions they don't like only at press conferences. But they hold few of them, and when they do, the questions are often quite mild out of fear that unwelcome questions invite punishment of the questioner.

Politicians would not get away with avoiding tough questions if the public demanded more scrutiny. Ultimately, it is up to the voters to punish those who dodge the media or unfairly attack the messenger by not voting for them.

KEEP IT BETWEEN THE DITCHES

Maintaining freedom of the press is much like driving on the highways. If you lean too far one way or the other, you will end up in a ditch.

Likewise, the pendulum of power between politicians and the media will never be in perfect posture. It will always be a moving target. But if we can keep it balanced somewhere near the center, the public is best served.

Attacking the media will always be great sport in our civic life. Real sports would be no fun at all if we could not yell at the referee or throw a hot dog at the umpire. But without them there wouldn't be a game.

Likewise, without a truly free and independent news media, there would be no democracy in America. So give the media "refs" a break. We screw up now and then, and we are trying to root out the bums, but most of us are doing our best to protect democracy, serve the public, and keep the game in play.

Appendix 1

Poll Watch:
Public Confidence in the Press

1972: Roper Center; Potomac Associates

Survey question: "How much trust and confidence do you have in the mass media—such as the newspapers, TV, and radio in general—when it comes to reporting the news fully, accurately, and fairly: A great deal, a fair amount, not very much, none at all?"

A great deal: 18%
A fair amount: 50%
Not very much: 24%
None at all: 6%

1974: Roper Center; Potomac Associates

Survey question: "How much trust and confidence do you have in the mass media—such as the newspapers, TV, and radio in general—when it comes to reporting the news fully, accurately, and fairly: A great deal, a fair amount, not very much, none at all?"

A great deal: 21%
A fair amount: 48%
Not very much: 21%
None at all: 8%

1976: Roper Center, Gallup, *Newsweek*
Survey question: "How much do you trust the news media?

A lot: 20%
Some: 66%
Not at all: 33%

1977: Roper Center: 11th Biennial Nationwide Study of Corporate Reputations
Survey question: "I would like your opinion on how much trust and confidence you have in news reporting on radio, TV, and in newspapers." (Respondents indicated their level of confidence by selecting a point on a scale of 1 to 7.)

High (6–7 points): 31%
Medium (3–5 points): 56%
Low (1–2 points): 13%

1979: Roper Center: 12th Biennial Nationwide Study of Corporate Reputations
Survey question: "I would like your opinion on how much trust and confidence you have in news reporting on radio, TV, and in newspapers."

High (6–7 points): 30%
Medium (3–5 points): 53%
Low (1–2 points): 16%

1981: Roper Center: Harris Survey
Survey question: "How must do you tend to trust . . . Washington news . . . that you see on television—very much, somewhat, or not very much?"

Very much: 21%
Somewhat: 58%
Not very much: 20%

1983: Roper Center: Public Opinion Index
Survey question: "I would like your opinion on how much trust and confidence you have in news reporting on radio, TV (television), and in newspapers."

High: 30%
Medium: 58%
Low: 12%

1984: Roper Center: General Social Survey
Survey question: "Would you say you have a great deal of confidence, only some confidence, or hardly any confidence at all in the press?"

A great deal: 17%
Only some: 59%
Hardly any: 22%

1986: Roper Center: General Social Survey
Survey question: "Would you say you have a great deal of confidence, only some confidence, or hardly any confidence at all in the press?"

A great deal: 18%
Only some: 54%
Hardly any: 26%

1988: Roper Center: General Social Survey
Survey question: "Would you say you have a great deal of confidence, only some confidence, or hardly any confidence at all in the press?"

A great deal: 18%
Only some: 53%
Hardly any: 25%

1992: Roper Center: CNN, Knight Ridder
Survey question: "Generally speaking, how often do you think you can trust each of the following to do what is right? Can you trust . . . the news media . . . most of the time, only some of the time, hardly ever or never?"

Most of the time: 26%
Only some: 48%
Hardly ever: 18%
Never: 8%

1994: Roper Center: Gallup Organization
Survey question: "Please tell me how much confidence you, yourself, have in media, such as newspapers, TV, radio—a great deal, quite a lot, some or very little?"

A great deal: 6%
Quite a lot: 20%
Some: 41%
Very little: 32%

1995: Roper Center: Princeton Survey Research
Survey question: "How much confidence do you have in the news media?"

A great deal: 6%
Quite a lot: 14%
Some: 40%
Very little: 37%

1997: Roper Center: Gallup

Survey question: "How much trust and confidence do you have in the mass media—such as the newspapers, TV, and radio in general—when it comes to reporting the news fully, accurately, and fairly: a great deal, a fair amount, not very much, none at all?"

Great deal: 10%
Fair amount: 43%
Not very much: 31%
None: 15%

1999: Roper Center: National Center for State Courts, Hearst Corp.

Survey question: "Would you say you have a great deal of confidence/trust, some confidence/trust, only a little confidence/trust, or no confidence/trust at all in the media?"

Great deal of confidence/trust: 10%
Some confidence/trust: 30%
Only a little confidence/trust: 31%
No confidence/trust at all: 18%

2000: Roper Center: ABC News, *Washington Post*

Survey question: "Would you say you have a great deal of confidence/trust, quite a lot of confidence/trust, some confidence/trust, very little confidence/trust, or no confidence/trust at all in the media?"

A great deal: 9%
Quite a lot: 15%
Some: 43%
Very little: 29%
None: 2%

2002: Roper Center: NBC News, *Wall Street Journal* Poll

Survey question: "Would you say you have a great deal of confidence/trust, quite a bit of confidence/trust, some confidence/trust, very little confidence/trust, or no confidence/trust at all in the national news media?"

> A great deal: 13%
> Quite a bit: 17%
> Some: 39%
> Very little: 19%
> None: 10%

2003: Roper Center: Program in International Policy Attitudes, University of Maryland

Survey question: "Would you say you have a lot of confidence/trust, some confidence/trust, not much confidence/trust, or no confidence/trust at all in the press and media?"

> A lot: 6%
> Some: 43%
> Not much: 32%
> None: 19%

2004: Roper Center: Gallup

Survey question: "In general, how much trust and confidence do you have in the mass media—such as newspapers, TV, and radio—when it comes to reporting the news fully, accurately and fairly—a great deal, a fair amount, not very much, or none at all?"

> Great deal: 9%
> Fair amount: 35%
> Not much: 39%
> None: 16%

Appendix 2

Media Resource Guide

MEDIA WATCHDOGS

Several media-monitoring groups exist to help news consumers guard against bias, but none is truly independent. These groups approach their analysis as ideologues who believe the media is biased against their point of view. But their work is useful. With untiring research, these watchdogs provide a comprehensive review of the news media's many failings.

Media Research Center
Brent Bozell, Chairman
325 South Patrick Street
Alexandria, VA 22314
Phone: 703-683-9733
www.mediaresearch.org

"The mission of the Media Research Center is to bring balance and responsibility to the news media. Leaders of America's conservative movement have long believed that within the national news media a strident liberal bias existed that influenced the public's understanding of critical issues. On October 1, 1987, a group of young determined conservatives set out to not only prove—through sound scientific research—that liberal bias in the media does exist and undermines traditional American values, but also to neutralize its impact on the American political scene. What they launched that fall is the now acclaimed."

—Media Research Center

Fairness and Accuracy In Reporting (FAIR)
Julie Hollar
112 West 27th Street
New York, NY 10001
Phone: 212-633-6700
Fax: 212-727-7668
www.fair.org

"FAIR, the national media watch group, has been offering well-documented criticism of media bias and censorship since 1986. We work to invigorate the First Amendment by advocating for greater diversity in the press and by scrutinizing media practices that marginalize public interest, minority and dissenting viewpoints. As an anti-censorship organization, we expose neglected news stories and defend working journalists when they are muzzled. As a progressive group, FAIR believes that structural reform is ultimately needed to break up the dominant media conglomerates, establish independent public broadcasting and promote strong non-profit sources of information."

—Fairness and Accuracy In Reporting

Accuracy In the Media (AIM)
Don Irvine, Director
4455 Connecticut Avenue NW
Suite 330
Washington, DC 20008
Phone: 202-364-4401
www.aim.org

"Accuracy In Media is a non-profit, grassroots citizens watchdog of the news media that critiques botched and bungled news stories and sets the record straight on important issues that have received slanted coverage."

—Accuracy In the Media

MEDIA ADVOCATES

The Reporters Committee for Freedom of the Press was founded by journalists to protect their First Amendment rights. The committee is usually at the center of any legal or political dispute involving freedom of the press.

Reporters Committee for Freedom of the Press
Lucy Dalglish
1101 Wilson Boulevard
Suite 1100
Arlington, VA 22209
Phone: 703-807-2100
www.rcfp.org

"The Reporters Committee for Freedom of the Press was created in 1970 at a time when the nation's news media faced a wave of government subpoenas asking reporters to name confidential sources. One case particularly galvanized American journalists. *New York Times* reporter Earl Caldwell was ordered to reveal to a federal grand jury his sources in the Black Panther organization, threatening his independence as a newsgatherer.

Caldwell's dilemma prompted a meeting at Georgetown University to discuss the need to provide legal assistance to journalists when their First Amendment rights come under fire. Among those present, or involved soon afterwards, were J. Anthony Lukas, Murray Fromson, Fred

Graham, Jack Nelson, Ben Bradlee, Eileen Shanahan, Mike Wallace, Robert Maynard and Tom Wicker. They formed a committee that operated part-time and on a shoestring (its first "office" was a desk in the press room at the U.S. Supreme Court). With support from foundations and news organizations, the founders built a staff and began recruiting attorneys to donate their services.

Almost immediately, the Committee waded into a number of free speech battles, intervening in court cases and fighting to keep Richard Nixon from retaining sole custody of his presidential papers. In the last two decades the Committee has played a role in virtually every significant press freedom case that has come before the Supreme Court—from Nebraska Press Association v. Stuart to Hustler Magazine v. Falwell—as well as in hundreds of cases in federal and state courts."

—Reporters Committee for Freedom of the Press

MEDIA THINK TANKS

Independent media research groups do exist. Mostly sponsored by universities or news organizations, they provide data and analysis about newsgathering trends, audience demographics, and other useful guides for evaluating the role of the media in society.

American Press Institute (API)
11690 Sunrise Valley Drive
Reston, VA 20191-1498
Phone: 703-620-3611
Contact: Andrew Nachison
www.americanpressinstitute.org
www.mediacenter.org/mediacenter/about/mission

"Founded by newspaper publishers in 1946, the American Press Institute is the oldest and largest center devoted solely to training and professional development for the news industry and journalism educators. The Institute, housed in a Marcel Breuer–designed building in Reston, Virginia, conducts more than 30 residential seminars a year for journalists, sales, marketing and management professionals in print, broadcast, cable and digital media companies. API has 'tracks' of programs in advertising, circulation, editorial, general management, marketing and weekly newspapers, while The Media Center focuses on a cross-section of professionals working in digital news, including online, wireless and new media."

—American Press Institute

American Journalism Review
University of Maryland
1117 Journalism Building
College Park, MD 20742-7111
Contact: Thomas Kunkel
http://ajr.org

"*American Journalism Review* is a national magazine that covers all aspects of print, television, radio and online media. The magazine, which is published six times a year, examines how the media cover specific stories and broader coverage trends. *AJR* analyzes ethical dilemmas in the field and monitors the impact of technology on how journalism is practiced and on the final product. The magazine is owned by the Philip Merrill College of Journalism at the University of Maryland."

—*American Journalism Review*

The Annenberg Public Policy Center
320 National Press Building
Washington, DC 20045
Phone: 202-879-6700
Contact: Kathleen Hall Jamieson, Ph.D., Director
www.annenbergpublicpolicycenter.org

"Established in 1994, the Annenberg Public Policy Center of the University of Pennsylvania conducts and disseminates research, hosts lectures and conferences, and convenes roundtable discussions that highlight important questions about the intersection of media, communication, and public policy. The Policy Center, which has offices in Philadelphia and Washington, DC, conducts ongoing research in the areas of political communication, information and society, media and the developing child, health communication, and adolescent risk. Its research helps to bring difficult problems into focus."

—Annenberg Public Policy Center

Center for Media and Public Affairs
2100 L Street NW
Suite 300
Washington, DC 20037
Phone: 202-223-2942
Contact: Dr. S. Robert Lichter
www.cmpa.com

"The Center for Media and Public Affairs (CMPA) is a nonpartisan research and educational organization which conducts scientific studies of the news and entertainment media. CMPA election studies have played a major role in the ongoing debate over improving the election process. Our continuing analysis and tabulation of late night political jokes provides a lighter look at major news makers. Since its formation in 1985, CMPA has emerged as a unique institution that bridges the gap between academic research and the broader domains of media and public policy. Founded by Drs. Robert and Linda Lichter, CMPA has become an acknowledged source of expertise in media analysis."

—Center for Media and Public Affairs

Pew Center for Civic Journalism
7100 Baltimore Avenue
Suite 101
College Park, MD 20740-3637
Phone: 301-985-4020
www.pewcenter.org

"The Pew Center for Civic Journalism was created by The Pew Chari-table Trusts to help stimulate citizen involvement in community issues. The project helps print and broadcast news organizations experiment with ways to reconnect to their communities and engage their citizens in dialogue and problem solving."

—Pew Center for Civic Journalism

Pew Research Center
1615 L Street NW
Suite 700
Washington, DC 20036
Phone: 202-419-4300
Contact: Andrew Kohut, President

"The Center is an independent opinion research group that studies attitudes toward the press, politics and public policy issues. We are best known for regular national surveys that measure public atten-tiveness to major news stories, and for our polling that charts trends in values and fundamental political and social attitudes. Formerly, the Times Mirror Center for the People & the Press (1990–1995), we are now sponsored by The Pew Charitable Trusts. The Center's pur-pose is to serve as a forum for ideas on the media and public policy through public opinion research. In this role it serves as an important information resource for political leaders, journalists, scholars, and public interest organizations. All of our current survey results are made available free of charge."

—Pew Research Center

The Poynter Institute
Karen Brown Dunlap, President
801 Third Street South
St. Petersburg, FL 33701
Phone: 888-769-6837
www.poynter.org

"The Poynter Institute is a school for journalists and leaders of news media. Poynter conducts more than 50 seminars annually in the areas of leadership and management, news reporting and writing, producing news for broadcast and online, ethics and diversity, and visual journalism. The school owns the Times Publishing Company, which publishes the *St. Petersburg Times*, and operates *Congressional Quarterly* and other publications."

—The Poynter Institute

Notes

CHAPTER 1: TURNING THE TABLES

1. "Rather's Questioning of Bush Sets Off Shouting on Live Broadcast," *New York Times*, January 26, 1988.

2. Thomas Jefferson: "The man who never looks into a newspaper is better informed than he who reads them, inasmuch as he who knows nothing is nearer to truth than he whose mind is filled with falsehoods and errors. He who reads nothing will still learn the great facts, and the details are all false. . . . Nothing can now be believed which is seen in a newspaper. Truth itself becomes suspicious by being put into that polluted vehicle. The real extent of this state of misinformation is known only to those who are in situations to confront facts within their knowledge with the lies of the day" (letter to John Norvell, 1807).

3. CBS News transcripts, January 25, 1988.

4. CBS News transcripts, January 25, 1988.

5. Interview with CBS camera operator George Christian, December 2, 2004.

6. Margaret Garrard Warner, "Bush Battles the Wimp Factor," *Newsweek*, October 19, 1987.

7. Ken Auletta, "Fortress Bush: How the White House Keeps the Press under Control," *The New Yorker*, January 19, 2004.

8. CBS News transcripts, January 25, 1988.

9. Interviews with CBS News personnel, November–December 2004.

10. CBS News transcripts, January 25, 1988.

11. Interviews with CBS News personnel, November–December 2004.

12. "Rather's Questioning of Bush Sets Off Shouting on Live Broadcast."

13. Interviews with CBS News personnel, November–December 2004.

14. "Rather's Questioning of Bush Sets Off Shouting on Live Broadcast."

15. Maureen Dowd, "Hometown Crowd Turns Tables on Press for Questioning Quayle," *New York Times*, August 19, 1988.

16. William Safire, "The Bush Dilemma," *New York Times*, August 22, 1988.

CHAPTER 2: BLAME THE MESSENGER

1. Yotam Barkai, "Dean '71 Criticizes News Media," *Yale Daily News*, November 17, 2004.

2. Don Imus, "Imus in the Morning," MSNBC, April 22, 2004.

3. "Nixon Concedes Defeat in Gubernatorial Election" (transcribed from audio file posted at www.historychannel.com), November 7, 1962.

4. "Nixon Concedes Defeat in Gubernatorial Election."

5. "Nixon Concedes Defeat in Gubernatorial Election."

6. Historian Charles A. Beard: "All the lessons of history in four sentences: Whom the gods would destroy, they first make mad with power. The mills of God grind slowly, but they grind exceedingly small. The bee fertilizes the flower it robs. When it is dark enough, you can see the stars." *Reader's Digest*, February 1941.

7. Beth Fouhy, "Major Network News Chiefs Review Election, Look to Future," Associated Press, November 16, 2004.

8. Fouhy, "Major Network News Chiefs Review Election, Look to Future."

9. Gallup Poll data.

10. Keith Olbermann, "Votes, Steroids, and Shoes," Bloggermann MSNBC.com, December 5, 2004.

11. James Wolcott, "Round Up the Cattle!," *Vanity Fair*, June 2003.

12. Helen E. Veit, Kenneth R. Bowling, and Charlene Bangs Bickford, *Creating the Bill of Rights: The Documentary Record from the First Federal Congress* (Baltimore: Johns Hopkins University Press, 1991).

CHAPTER 3: A PRESIDENT LIES

1. Sources for this section and the following two of this chapter: Ron Fournier, "Clinton Angrily Denies Allegations," Associated Press, January 26, 1998; Sandra Sobieraj, "Clinton's Denial a Stern 20-Seconds," Associated Press, January 26, 1998; Pete Yost, "Clinton: I Didn't Have Sex with Her," Associated Press, January 26, 1998; Bill Nichols and Kevin Johnson, "Clinton Issues Angry Denial," *USA Today*, January 27, 1998; Arthur Brice, "President Passionate in Denying Allegations," *Atlanta Journal-Constitution*, January 27, 1998; Carl M. Cannon, "Clinton Pounds Fist while Denying He Had Sex with Lewinsky," *Baltimore Sun*, January 27, 1998; Brian McGrory, "President Issues His Strongest Denial Yet," *Boston Globe*, January 27, 1998; David Bianculli, "Networks Bobbled Clinton's Retort," *New York Daily News*, January 27, 1998; "Clinton Denial: Characterizations," *The Hotline*, January 27, 1998; James Bennet, "The President under Fire," *New York Times*, January 27, 1998.

2. Ron Fournier, "Clinton Angrily Denies Allegations," Associated Press, January 26, 1998.

3. Transcript of Clinton remarks at after-school program event, U.S. Newswire, January 27, 1998.

4. Sandra Sobieraj, "Clinton's Denial a Stern 20-Seconds," Associated Press, January 26, 1998.

5. Sources for this section: Renee Loth, "Bush's Denial of Infidelity Rumor Sparks Stories, Déjà Vu," *Boston Globe*, August 13, 1992; Frank J. Murray, "'Sleaze' Question Angers President," *Washington Times*, August 12, 1992; Tom Raum, "Bush Denies Report of Affair but Rebuffs Question on Adultery," Associated Press, August 11, 1992; Howard Kurtz, "Bush Angrily Denounces Report of Extramarital Affair," *Washington Post*, August 12, 1992; James Gerstenzang, "President Denounces as a Lie Paper's Story of Romantic Affair," *Los Angeles Times*, August 12, 1992; John W. Mashek and Walter V. Robinson, "Angry Bush Calls Affair Story 'a Lie'; Scolds Reporters for Asking about New York Post Report Alleging 1984 Liaison," *Boston Globe*, August 12, 1992; "Bush Text on Family Questions," *The Hotline*, August 12, 1992; transcript of White House press briefing by Mike McCurry, U.S. Newswire, January 27, 1998.

6. Sobieraj, "Clinton's Denial a Stern 20-Seconds."

7. Transcript of White House press briefing by Mike McCurry, U.S. Newswire, January 27, 1998.

8. Roger Simon, "Clinton Vehemently Denies the Charges," *Chicago Tribune*, January 27, 1998.

9. Paul Bedard, "No 'Sexual Relations,'" *Washington Times*, January 27, 1998.

10. Simon, "Clinton Vehemently Denies the Charges."

11. Jim Nolan, "Dissection of Prez's Statement Has Begun," *Philadelphia Daily News*, January 27, 1998.

12. Rita Delfiner, "Gesture Experts Look for 'Body' of Evidence," *New York Post*, January 27, 1998.

CHAPTER 4: SPINNING LIES

1. Mark Twain, *Following the Equator: A Journey around the World* (reprint, New York: Dover Publications, 1989), chapter 7.

2. Aaron Sorkin, *A Few Good Men* (New York: Samuel French Inc Plays, 1991).

3. Transcript of July 15, 1979, speech by President Jimmy Carter, Program in Presidential Rhetoric, Texas A&M University, Department of Communication (accessed online at www.tamu.edu).

4. Larry Sabato quote: Tom Raum, "Newsview: Political Rhetoric Has Price," Associated Press, November 27, 2004.

5. Interview, Clinton cabinet member, November 2004.

6. Bob Deans, "Sticking Up for the Boss; President Sends Out Cabinet Officials to Insist He's Not a Liar," *Atlanta Journal-Constitution*, January 24, 1998.

7. "Propaganda," *Britannica Student Encyclopedia* (Encyclopedia Britannica Online, 2003).

8. David Dowd, "Art as National Propaganda in the French Revolution," *Public Opinion Quarterly* 15 (autumn 1951): 532.

9. Jane DeRose Evans, *The Art of Persuasion: Political Propaganda from Aeneas to Brutus* (Ann Arbor: University of Michigan Press, 1992).

10. Sources for this section: Michael Isikoff, "Drug Buy Set Up for Bush Speech; DEA Lured Seller to Lafayette Park," *Washington Post*, September 22,

1989; David Hoffman, "Bush Defends Luring Drug Suspect; Sen. Breaux Criticizes 'Theatrics' in Use of Cocaine as Prop," *Washington Post*, September 23, 1989; Tracy Thompson and Michael Isikoff, "Lafayette Square Drug Suspect Indicted," *Washington Post*, September 27, 1989.

11. Political television ad analysis: Annenberg Public Policy Center, University of Pennsylvania (accessed online at www.FactCheck.org).

12. Political television ad analysis: Annenberg Public Policy Center, University of Pennsylvania (accessed online at www.FactCheck.org).

13. Political television ad analysis: Annenberg Public Policy Center, University of Pennsylvania (accessed online at www.FactCheck.org).

14. Transcript of October 13, 2004, presidential debate in Tempe, Arizona, Commission on Presidential Debates.

15. Sources for the Halperin discussion: Howard Kurtz, "Balance in a Spinning World," *Washington Post*, October 18, 2004; "The Halperin Memo: ABC & Liars" (editorial), *Pittsburgh Tribune Review*, October 13, 2004; Greg Pierce, "Inside Politics: The ABC Memo," *Washington Times*, October 13, 2004; John Podhoretz, "Smoking Gun—ABC's of Media Bias," *New York Post*, October 12, 2004; Peter Johnson, "Are the Media Playing Politics?" *USA Today*, October 11, 2004.

CHAPTER 5: A WAR STORY

1. Transcript of press briefing by Ari Fleischer, 2003 Federal Information and News Dispatch, Inc., March 18, 2004.

2. Interview with Helen Thomas, April 15, 2004.

3. Transcript of press briefing by Ari Fleischer, 2003 Federal Information and News Dispatch, Inc., March 18, 2004.

4. Interview with Helen Thomas, April 15, 2004.

5. Interviews with former cable television news anchor and producer, November 2003.

6. Interviews with former cable television news anchor and producer, November 2003.

7. Thomas Jefferson: "I deplore . . . the putrid state into which our newspapers have passed and the malignity, the vulgarity, and mendacious spirit of those who write for them. . . . These ordures are rapidly depraving the public

taste and lessening its relish for sound food. As vehicles of information and a curb on our functionaries, they have rendered themselves useless by forfeiting all title to belief. . . . This has, in a great degree, been produced by the violence and malignity of party spirit" (letter to Walter Jones, 1814, *The Writings of Thomas Jefferson* [Washington, D.C., 1903–1904]).

8. Jefferson, letter to Walter Jones, 1814.

9. Roy P. Basler, ed., *The Collected Works of Abraham Lincoln*, vol. 7 (New Brunswick, N.J.: Rutgers University Press, 1953), 347–48, accessed online at www.hti.umich.edu (letter to John A. Dix, May 18, 1864).

10. James Ford Rhodes, *History of the United States* (New York: Macmillan, 1902).

11. Ann Coulter, "This Is War," *National Review*, September 13, 2001.

12. Craig Crawford, "Democrats Hold Fire on Criticizing Bush War Plan," *CQ Today*, March 28, 2003.

13. Crawford, "Democrats Hold Fire on Criticizing Bush War Plan."

14. Crawford, "Democrats Hold Fire on Criticizing Bush War Plan."

15. Colman McCarthy, "TV's Military 'Embeds,'" *Washington Post*, April 19, 2003.

16. Jim Rutenberg, "Ex-Generals Defend Their Blunt Comments," *New York Times*, April 2, 2003.

CHAPTER 6: WHO WILL TELL THE TRUTH?

1. "And ye shall know the truth, and the truth shall make you free," New Testament (King James Version, John 8:32).

2. Steven Winn, "A Nation Trusted Him. And He Has Never Betrayed That Trust. We're Still Listening to Walter Cronkite," *San Francisco Chronicle*, March 2, 2004.

3. Television audience data, Pew Research Center for the People and the Press, Washington, D.C.

4. Walter Cronkite, "We Are Mired in Stalemate," *CBS Evening News* transcript, February 27, 1968.

5. Presidential Address to the Nation, March 31, 1968, *Public Papers of the Presidents of the United States: Lyndon B. Johnson, 1968–69*, vol. 1 (Washington, D.C.: U.S. Government Printing Office, 1970), 469–76.

6. President Lyndon Johnson's May 27, 1964, telephone conversation with National Security Adviser McGeorge Bundy, audiotape (LBJ Library, Austin, Texas).

7. Dana Milbank, "Curtains Ordered for Media Coverage of Returning Coffins," *Washington Post*, October 21, 2003.

8. Bryan Bender, "For Those Receiving US Dead, a Test of Faith," *Boston Globe*, April 12, 2004.

9. Hal Bernton, "Woman Loses Her Job over Coffins Photo," *Seattle Times*, April 22, 2004.

10. Hal Bernton and Ray Rivera, "How Two Women, One Photo Stirred National Debate," *Seattle Times*, April 25, 2004.

11. Nicole Brodeur, "Picture's Imprint Won't Fade," *Seattle Times*, July 18, 2004.

CHAPTER 7: THE END OF AN ERA

1. "Dan Rather to Retire in March," *CBS Evening News* transcript, November 23, 2004.

2. Jacques Steinberg and Bill Carter, "Rather Quitting as CBS Anchor in Abrupt Move," *New York Times*, November 24, 2004.

3. Bill Carter, "Courage, CBS News," *New York Times*, November 24, 2004; Mark Jurkowitz and Renee Graham, "24-Year Anchor Rather to Depart," *Boston Globe*, November 24, 2004; Dan Glaister, "One of America's Most Venerable Broadcasters Is Stepping Down," *The Guardian* (London), November 26, 2004; Paul Brownfield, "Rather Exits; Is the End Near? News Faces Its Own Obit," *Los Angeles Times*, November 24, 2004.

4. "Documents Raise New Questions about President Bush's Service in the Texas Air National Guard," *CBS Evening News* transcript, September 8, 2004; "Bush Administration Reacts to Documents Which Raise Questions about President Bush's Military Service," *CBS Evening News* transcript, September 8, 2004.

5. "New Records Raise Questions about President Bush's National Guard Service," *CBS Evening News* transcript, September 9, 2004; "Questions Raised about CBS News Report regarding President Bush's Time in the National Guard," *CBS Evening News* transcript, September 9, 2004.

6. "Documents Used in a CBS Report on President Bush's Texas Air National Guard Service Are Being Questioned by Some Experts and Defended by Others," *CBS Evening News* transcript, September 13, 2004; "CBS News Draws Fire from Reports Raising Questions regarding President Bush's National Guard Service," *CBS Evening News* transcript, September 15, 2004; "For the Record; Marion Carr Knox, Former Secretary to Colonel Jerry Killian, Discusses George Bush Memos," transcript of CBS News' *60 Minutes*, September 15, 2004.

7. "CBS News Admits to Being Misled regarding Documents Pertaining to President Bush's National Guard Service," transcript of CBS News' *60 Minutes*, September 20, 2004.

8. Steinberg and Carter, "Rather Quitting as CBS Anchor in Abrupt Move."

9. "Dan Rather to Retire in March," *CBS Evening News* transcript, November 23, 2004.

10. Mark Jurkowitz, "PBS Anchor Chides Big 3 Networks as Shirking Convention Duty," *Boston Globe*, July 26, 2004.

CHAPTER 8: WINNERS AND LOSERS

1. Louis W. Liebovich, *The Press and the Modern Presidency: Myths and Mindsets from Kennedy to Election 2000* (Westport, Conn.: Praeger Publishers, 2001).

2. Yotam Barkai, "Dean '71 Criticizes News Media," *Yale Daily News*, November 17, 2004.

3. Ken Auletta, "Fortress Bush: How the White House Keeps the Press under Control," *The New Yorker*, January 19, 2004.

4. "Missing the Evidence on Missing Explosives," Fairness and Accuracy in Reporting, October 29, 2004 (accessed online at www.fair.org/press-releases/missing-explosives.html).

5. James Glanz, William J. Broad, and David E. Sanger, "Huge Cache of Explosives Vanished from Site in Iraq," *New York Times*, October, 25, 2004.

6. "Missing Weapons Iraq Munitions Scandal," *ABC World News Tonight* transcript, October 28, 2004; "Soldiers Who Entered Site of Missing Iraq Explosives Conducted Only Cursory Search: Commander," Agence France-Presse, October 27, 2004.

7. Mark Mazzetti, "News Video Is at Center of Storm over Iraq Explosives; Reporters Taped Troops Apparently Finding Munitions. A Pentagon Photo Implies Otherwise," *Los Angeles Times*, October 29, 2004.

8. Bradley Graham and Thomas E. Ricks, "Munitions Issue Dwarfs the Big Picture," *Washington Post*, October 29, 2004.

9. "Bush and Kerry Continue Stinging Exchange on Missing Weapons," *Special Report* transcript, Fox News Channel, October 28, 2004.

10. Maura Reynolds and Michael Finnegan, "Munitions Issue Cuts Both Ways," *Los Angeles Times*, October, 29, 2004.

11. "News Audiences Increasingly Politicized," Pew Research Center study, released June 8, 2004 (available online at www.people-press.org).

12. Noam Chomsky, *Media Control: The Spectacular Achievements of Propaganda* (New York: Seven Stories Press, 1997).

CHAPTER 9: MEDIA CULPA

1. "News Media's Improved Image Proves Short-Lived," Pew Research Center for the People and the Press, August 4, 2002.

2. Joseph Carroll, "Honesty Ratings of Pharmacists, State Officeholders Reach New Highs; Image of Military Officers, Day Care Providers Also More Positive," Gallup News Service, December 8, 2004.

3. Craig Crawford, "After 18 Months of Watching, It's Time to Predict," *CQ Today*, October 22, 2004.

4. David Shaw, "When the Journalism Itself Was the Bad News," *Los Angeles Times*, December 19, 2004.

CHAPTER 10: HOW TO GET THE REAL STORY

1. Frazier Moore, "Bill Moyers Retiring from TV Journalism," Associated Press, December 9, 2004. Moyers: "We have an ideological press that's interested in the election of Republicans, and a mainstream press that's interested in the bottom line. Therefore, we don't have a vigilant, independent press whose interest is the American people."

2. Transcript of interview with NBC's Brian Williams, C-SPAN, December 26, 2004 (accessed online at www.c-span.org).

3. David Bauder, "Does Backlash Loom against Opinion News?," Associated Press, November 14, 2004.

4. Anick Jesdanun, "Broadband Use Surpasses Dial-Up in U.S.," Associated Press, December 21, 2004.

5. Howard Kurtz, "Washington Post Buys Microsoft's Webzine," *Washington Post*, December 22, 2004.

CHAPTER 11: WHAT NOW?

1. Larry Sabato, *Feeding Frenzy* (New York: Free Press, 1993).

2. Peter Johnson, "Media Have Become the Message in a Bruising Political Year," *USA Today*, October 25, 2004.

3. "*Slate* Votes: At This Magazine, It's Kerry by a Landslide!," *Slate* (www.slate.msn.com), October 26, 2004. Editor Jacob Weisberg: "News organizations that, for understandable reasons, are less open about the political views of their staff may have a harder time with the challenge of being fair to both sides. Repressed politics, like repressed sexuality, tends to find an outlet of one kind or another."

4. Dr. Ink, "Afflicting the Afflicted, a Wise Saying Contorted," Poynter Institute online (www.poynter.org), April 24, 2002. Finley Peter Dunne as "Mr. Dooley" (in Irish dialect): "Th' newspaper does ivrything f'r us. It runs th' polis foorce an' th' banks, commands th' milishy, controls th'ligislachure, baptizes th' young, marries th' foolish, comforts th' afflicted, afflicts th' comfortable, buries th' dead an' roasts thim aftherward."

Index

About the Author

Craig Crawford is one of Washington, D.C.'s, most popular news commentators; his wit and wisdom are featured almost daily on national television and radio programs including *The Early Show* on CBS, various programs on CNBC and MSNBC including *Countdown with Keith Olbermann* and *Hardball*, and CBS Network radio. A White House columnist for *Congressional Quarterly*, he is also a frequent commentator for *NBC Nightly News*, *CBS Evening News*, and *Imus in the Morning*. Before joining *Congressional Quarterly*, Crawford ran *The Hotline*, an online news digest that is an institution inside the Beltway and out. Before coming to Washington, Crawford practiced law in Florida and was a reporter for the *Orlando Sentinel*. He also once ran for a state legislative seat in Orlando, so he has seen both sides of the story he tells here. Although no longer practicing, he is still a licensed attorney in the Florida Bar. He currently lives in Washington, D.C., and was hailed by the *Washington Post* as "one of the capital's most celebrated journalists" in a profile published May 18, 2000.

AMERICAN POLITICAL CHALLENGES
Larry J. Sabato, *Series Editor*

The American political process is in trouble. Although we witnessed a movement toward specific electoral reforms in the aftermath of the 2000 election debacle and in the run-up to 2004, the health of our political system is still at risk. Recent events have altered the political landscape and posed new challenges, and reforms are much needed and wanted by the American public. Diligence is required, however, in examining carefully the intended and unintended consequences of reforms—such as BCRA—as we look toward the 2006 elections and beyond.

Series Editor Larry J. Sabato of the University of Virginia Center for Politics is a leading political scientist and commentator who has clear ideas about what needs to change to improve the quality of our democracy. For this series, he taps leading political authors to write cogent diagnoses and prescriptions for improving both politics and government. New and forthcoming books in the series are short, to the point, and easy to understand (if difficult to implement against the political grain). They take a stand and show how to overcome obstacles to change. Authors are known for their clear writing style as well as for their political acumen.

Titles in the Series

Chesapeake Bay Blues: Science, Politics, and the Struggle to Save the Bay
  Howard R. Ernst

The Pursuit of Happiness in Times of War
  Carl M. Cannon

The Presidential Nominating Process: A Place for Us?
  Rhodes Cook

Freedom Is Not Enough: Black Voters, Black Candidates, and American Presidential Politics
  Ronald W. Walters

Attack the Messenger: How Politicians Turn You against the Media
  Craig Crawford